Coloring Outside the Lines

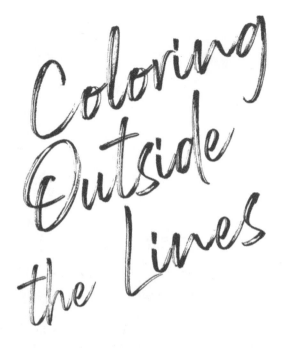

Coloring Outside the Lines

MY JOURNEY TO ABLE LIVING IN A DISABLED BODY

J. WALTON

MYND MATTERS

Published by
Mynd Matters Publishing
715 Peachtree Street NE, Suites 100 & 200
Atlanta, GA 30308
www.myndmatterspublishing.com

978-1-953307-14-9 (Pbk)
978-1-953307-15-6 (eBook)

FIRST EDITION

A special thanks to
God, my family, Paula, Erica, Fay, Linda and Vicki.

Contents

Introduction

It all started with an ad that read something like:

WANTED:
A MATURE WOMAN DEDICATED TO HELPING STUDENT WITH A DISABILITY GO TO SCHOOL AND PERFORM DAILY LIVING ACTIVITIES.

This might sound like one of those "dummy" ads trying to entice innocent readers into joining a swinger's relationship. And to be honest, I am sure that is why we received some interesting replies. However, my parents had something totally different in mind when they placed the ad in various newspapers around town and throughout multiple states. No matter how old I was, my parents kept hoping that Mary Poppins was just around the corner, ready to keep me in tiptop shape. I found it fortunate no such person ever showed up on our doorstep.

The anticipation and total anxiety I felt each time the ad was placed in a newspaper was excruciating. That small ad had the potential to lead me to a series of total strangers with whom I could possibly share some of the greatest adventures of my life. Alternately, the same could be true in reverse. Millions of questions would stir in my mind for weeks before each initial face-to-face meeting. Important questions such as, *Does she like to eat? Will she eat her own cooking? Will she have a good sense of humor or will she look at me as my mother so often did, with total amazement, disgust or disbelief, when she could not figure out my thoughts or actions? Will I soon see her profiled on America's Most Wanted because of the bang-up job she did as the Merry Machine Gun Closet Murderer?"*

These, and other stomach-churning questions, were eventually answered as each new personal assistant and I got to know one another.

As you can probably tell by now, this ad was used to attract nice, unsuspecting women to be my personal assistant for a period of time to help me accomplish daily living skills. It took a great deal of blind faith and courage to answer "the call" of this ad on the part of everyone concerned. When a good match was made, both of our lives were abundantly enriched by the experiences we shared. When our personalities did not match so well, we still gained knowledge from our time together. At times we gained much more than either of us bargained for!

Looking back on those times in my life, I cannot help but truly believe that my disability, in combination with blind faith and this innocent ad, led me to engage in the abundant life that God meant for all of us to have. In the gospel of John 10:10, Jesus says, "The thief (Satan) comes only to steal and kill and destroy, I (Jesus) came that we may have life, and have it more abundantly." Who knows how many times I have quickly glazed over this verse like a Krispy Kreme donut without thoroughly digesting or thinking about what He was telling us. But one day it struck me like a bolt of lightning that this verse does not mean Jesus came so that our lives would be abundantly joyous, happy, or even easy. It says that He came so that we may have more of an abundant life. The special women who answered the simple ad indeed enabled me to experience abundance through a series of escapades and adventures in a disabled body.

You will discover soon enough, that I am far from a Greek philosopher, but have you ever stopped to think about what life is made of? To me, life is one huge bag full of mixed nuts made up of both births and deaths, joy and sadness, settled and uncertain times, health and sickness, hunger, satisfaction, pride, humiliation, strong beliefs and total disbelief, victories, defeats, and every other state of being under the sun. If the proper definition for "abundant" is full, existing in plentiful supply, ample, and Jesus came into the world so that we might have life more abundantly, wouldn't it make sense that God would allow us to experience more of every aspect of life? This unfortunately includes even the unpleasant times where we would much rather skim off the top than bite down and chew.

We may sometimes experience both feast and famine at the same point in our abundant life. For instance, the birth of a child is a time of blissful wonder, a time to marvel at the great joy a newborn brings to a family. But when that baby, so perfect on the outside, is diagnosed with a debilitating condition, the time of joy can turn into devastation as we ponder the imperfect beginning of the child and the uncertainty that lies ahead. On a spiritual level we may question why this is happening. Financially, we may question the vast expense for what lies ahead. Worst of all, times such as these can feel like a withdrawal of God's presence and love. It feels that the more you look for Him to "stop the madness" and ease your pain, the more He chooses those times to perform a grand disappearing act. You may feel totally helpless and even betrayed because you thought God loved you enough not to put you in a situation like this. But often, these are some of the very times we look back and clearly see God's wonderful handiwork splattered intricately, purposefully on the painting of our life.

I have not been blessed with my own children so I cannot fathom what it feels like to raise your own flesh and blood then watch them struggle just to live an ordinary life, or to bury them due to an untimely death. But I have felt the horror and pure desperation of losing precious ones in my life. Many of you will laugh and think to yourselves, "Oh girl, that ain't nothing compared to the grief I've gone through!" But stay with me as I paint a picture to try and illustrate my point.

My personal assistant and I had two beloved Boxer dogs, Bogie and Bacall. As the lyrics to a 1980s pop song said,

"They had it all, just like Bogie and Bacall." As audacious as it sounds, you would be hard pressed to find two dogs or a litter of puppies that were more beloved than them. You see, these pups came along at the same time my biological clock was ticking and my personal assistant at the time, Halie, was suffering from an acute case of "empty nest syndrome." We totally lived and breathed Boxers for eight months straight and thoroughly enjoyed it. It was the only time in life when I did not mind getting out of my warm bed at 5:00 a.m. to let them out or mopping up their messes at least six times a day! Instead of a witch riding a broom, I was riding a mop through the house with the help of my electric wheelchair.

As all crazed "dog parents" do, we had grandiose dreams of raising the next American Kennel Club champion of the century, or at least the most beautiful Boxers in the world, and seeing their faces on various magazines throughout the country. When the puppies were six months old, we decided to take them running in the country. It was the best solution we could come up with to avoid turning our nice home into a dog pound. The plan was to follow along behind them in a little dune buggy. But sometimes the best-laid plans can turn tragic in the blink of an eye, leaving you speechless except for one word: why? That warm spring afternoon when Halie and I took the family out for a run in the country will replay in my mind like a bad nightmare for years to come. We let them out in the back pasture because we felt confident that we could keep track of the "fabulous four" at all times. As quickly as a steering wheel turns, my world too was turned upside down and inside out. Bacall and her two pups dearly loved chasing rabbits and were relentless once they caught the scent. That day, they must have caught the scent of *several* rabbits and scattered into the wind. Bogie came back immediately and my female puppy Godiva returned five days later with a gunshot wound to her jaw, in critical condition, but alive. Bacall and her son Phantom vanished without a trace.

For five days and six months afterwards, we did everything physically possible to find our dogs. Family and friends took hours out of their busy days driving around town in hopes of getting to the bottom of what had happened. For months we used resources like posters, TV and radio ads, web sites, and word of mouth to no avail. I have never felt more helpless in all my life. This heart wrenching experience helped me better understand how the loss of a loved can leave a significant hole in one's life.

Pain and anger are best friends. It's not unusual to have one without the other popping in and setting up camp for a while. When they enter the picture, it feels as if trouble comes packing a double punch. The previous two years, before I lost my dogs, had not been all that great for me either. My beloved grandmother, who was a delightfully loving source of humorous support in my early years, died. My parents divorced after thirty-eight years of marriage. Their separation greatly challenged my beliefs about love and security. Jackson, a dear mentor of mine, also suddenly died in an accident I felt was needless and preventable. My friendship with Halie, the personal assistant I believed I was going to grow old with, was steadily losing traction, and headed downhill fast and furiously. After working diligently for three years to complete a master's degree in counseling, I could not find a job. And then, on top of all that, I lost my dogs who were the closest thing to children I had ever known. I could not believe that God would not grant me such a seemingly small and inconsequential request such as keeping a family of silly Boxers. Pain and anger moved into the place where joy and happiness should have been and refused to be evicted.

One night after the dogs had been gone for five days and nights, I was preparing to invite God to my grand, old-fashioned, deluxe pity-party to ask Him why I was in this situation. Fortunately, *He* was saved by the bell. My youngest sister, who is wise beyond her years, called to ask how I was holding up. Her concern opened the floodgates of a hour-long pity party that culminated with this pronouncement: "I just cannot do this anymore!" Suddenly, I was struck with an epiphany that felt like the heavenly version of a two by four. As many times as Halie and I prayed for "our kids" to return, drove down the same streets and roads over and over, made phone calls, obsessively checked our message machine, the effort we exerted was absolutely nothing compared to the lengths Jesus Christ will go to in order to give us eternal life. The kind of life that He offers is much more abundant than we could ever dream. He will always leave the light on to find us no matter where we are or what our situation is.

This book is written with the hope of opening your eyes to the abundance all around. Having a disability may not be the easiest way to go through life, but it is far from the worst thing that can happen. Whether a person is born with a disability or develops one later in life, it is a very natural reaction to mourn over potential missed opportunities. It's like an "invasion" that not only affects the disabled person, but has a ripple effect on the individuals they know.

Think about it. No sane person, if given a choice, would openly invite a disability into his or her life. The feelings that manifested that horrible week after our dogs disappeared was a culmination of two prior years of sadness and unwise choices. God used that time to allow me to be invaded with sorrow, disbelief, and anger so I would stop and change the lines in the picture I was drawing for myself to live by. His infinite wisdom knew that guiding me to, and through, that horrible time was the most effective way to get my attention so I would consider that He might have abundantly more in store for me than what I had in store for myself. If invading one's life with a disability is what it takes for someone to know God's love and plans for them, then He will use it to give them abundantly more than they had ever thought possible.

Finding out you or a loved one is going to have to cope with a disability for the rest of life may be the hardest piece of news you will ever have to accept. Living with a disability and accepting one are two different paintings. We can live with a disability day after day and never accept it because of our preconceived notion of how life should be. Believe it or not, a disability is considered a "natural" occurrence in society, but it rarely feels natural. Depending on the severity and circumstances surrounding a person's condition, some are "denied" opportunities to participate in various activities that come along naturally with age. Basic simple life activities, such as driving a car, participating in meaningful relationships, having a family, or getting a job may be out of the question for some because of physical and/or mental limitations. This can be very demoralizing because it is always easy to find someone who has more than we do or has an easier life than ours. By comparing ourselves to others, we set ourselves up into thinking that our lives fall short of what it's "supposed" to be. A disability certainly does not fit into the lines that most people draw for themselves to live by.

When we were young, one of the best ways my parents kept my sisters and I quietly occupied was with paper and a box of crayons. We would carefully draw or trace a picture and then spend hours coloring in great detail. The spasticity that goes along with the type of cerebral palsy that I have would cause my hand to fling wildly across the page or color in tiny squiggles. No matter how hard I tried to color inside the lines, I just couldn't do it. This was very frustrating because my two younger sisters seemed to be able to create vivid pictures without much effort. There's nothing like a good case of sibling rivalry to motivate creativity. I finally started extending outlines to fit around the many "oops" that I made. So what if every face I drew resembled the Hunchback of Notre Dame? The colors all fit within the lines.

I think it's fair to assume that most artists have an idea of the outcome they want to achieve before they create their masterpiece. But the finished product may be very different from the way they imagined it. As the artist accommodates for a few "oopsies" in the project, it might be necessary to color outside some of the lines that were drawn in the original plan. Changing a line or shading with different colors may pull out different perspectives in a painting and create a masterpiece more abundantly beautiful than initially imagined.

Life can be this way. A disability can cause a person to contract their goals in some areas and expand in others beyond the outlines or limits they have set for themselves. I have cerebral palsy. It's a developmental, neurological disorder that affects my physical abilities, but my parents made sure that it had minimal impact on my mental abilities. They were always hoping that my disability would have a minimizing effect on the amount of mischief that I could get into, but as the following snapshots of my life will show, it did not. If anything, my disability has added a unique, comical side to my life that only could be experienced because of it.

Cerebral palsy added a twist to life that continuously

makes me color outside of my lines and enables me to experience life more abundantly with people than would probably be possible otherwise. This twist is what I like to call one of God's "little ironies." The disability that seemingly made me so incomplete at birth has in all actuality made me complete and unique. It's because of the personal assistants who have helped me out along the way. Some have stayed longer and remained close friends, while others stayed until they received a better offer. No matter the length of time we spent together, each one made a lasting impression on my life.

There are so many places this book could start from that it's hard to know where to begin. As you read about some of the funniest, most embarrassing times in my life, I truly hope that it brings you the kind of joy I've experienced alongside the special people God has brought into my life. Hopefully you'll see having a disability that makes one "color outside the lines," in the light Christ radiates, can easily lead to *Able Living in a Disabled Body.*

All names have been changed to protect the innocent and not so innocent. This book was written to point out the lighter side of my life and is by no means intended to disrespect or offend anyone or any group affiliations.

Chapter 1
1981-1982

Have you been driving long?

Remember the ad from earlier? It was placed in several newspapers in metropolitan areas in Texas, Oklahoma, and California. We chose these states because we had family members and/or close friends there who helped with the laborious task of the first screening before we made the long trek to meet the interviewee. Since many of these lucky people had known me even before I was born, they had a pretty good idea of what I needed, and the type of person my parents were looking for. Some of you have undoubtedly heard the saying, "It takes a village to raise a child." Well, it took the input of several states to raise me! The beginning of my junior year in high school was drawing near and that meant it was time to panic. My close friend Jewels, who had been a constant companion for several summers, was about to leave for college, so the search for a new victim or, shall I say in more politically correct terms, "personal assistant" was at full speed. No one answered the ad for several consecutive weeks, so my mother did what she does best in these situations. She called all family members and anyone that she had ever met in the last twenty years to see if they would donate a year of their time or, recommend a friend who would perhaps make a suitable personal assistant for me. As the ad said, the job description included making sure that I attended all of my classes, helping me complete assignments, and functioning as my hands and feet. It was also my parents' deep wish that the person keep me on the straight and narrow path of good behavior while also helping me do *some* crazy "age appropriate activities." This task alone was quite a handful for even the most capable.

The picture of mom sitting behind her roll-top desk, phone propped on her shoulder, anxiously jotting down the names and numbers of possible candidates with one hand while anchoring the pad of paper with the other, will always be burned into my memory. Her platinum blond hair was almost always neatly pulled up in a bun to keep it out of her stoic green eyes, which would be staring intently at the list of potential "victims." Sometimes it looked as if she was getting some kind of vibe or "insight" into a name by tapping her pencil over it. Thankfully my cousin came to the rescue with the "lucky connection" and stopped this mad hunt for an assistant.

Many of us have had the fascinating experience of being

set up on a blind date. If it turns out well, we are grateful to the one who made it happen. But, if it turns out to be a disaster, we're torn between feelings of disbelief and revenge. Our thoughts run amuck as we try to imagine how someone we thought knew us so well could fail us so badly as a matchmaker. When a blind date goes bad, we often wish that we had been "stood up" rather than "set up." When my cousin called and told us that a co-worker had a very nice niece who was interested in working with me, it felt as if I was being set up on a blind date—only worse. My mind immediately raced into third gear. Had I played any practical jokes on my cousin as we were growing up? Did I remember to send all the thank you notes my mother had nagged me about sending for years? I am an interesting combination of my parents. *Interesting can be a good or bad word, depending on the circumstances.* Volumes could be written about my mom's uncompromising, tenacious spirit that helped mold me into the uncompromising, tenacious person I am today. But one event is clearly book-marked in my memory.

It was the time mom was recuperating from a major surgery. I was worried about her recovery, so you would think that I would be totally focused on her needs at that time, but life rarely turns out the way I plan. It just so happened that on the same day mom came home from the hospital, my own personal crisis was brewing in the form of a stolen purse. My new assistant, Tricia had her purse stolen with my wallet inside while we were in the nurse's restroom at school. We'd assumed Tricia's purse was a safer place to keep my money than my book bag because I would lose my backside if it weren't attached to my body. My mom has that very annoying gift with which all mothers seem to be especially wired. She took one look at my face and knew something was amiss. Mom was *better* than a fortune teller. After several attempts to get me to spill the beans, I burst into tears and explained what had happened. Mom jumped on the case like an action figure jumps into action to solve "the mystery of the day." She asked the usual investigative questions about the scene of the 'crime' as she struggled to prop herself up with overstuffed pillows in my parents' king sized bed. If mom had one of those old-fashioned Smith-Corona typewriters in her lap, she could have passed for one of her favorite actresses, Jessica Lansbury in *Murder She Wrote*. A slightly less formal Jessica Lansbury, but one nonetheless.

Mom sternly asked for the phone book to find the school's number even though Tricia and I both attempted to convince her to forget about it because we could handle it. I knew it was futile and unwise to argue when she made up her mind to solve a problem. Secretly, I was glad she wanted to come to our rescue because I was sure she would either get the ball rolling or heads would soon be rolling. I was right. The next day, everyone from the principal to the janitorial staff had full knowledge of "our" purse and its contents.

Mysteriously, the purse magically reappeared at the scene of the crime not long afterwards. All our pictures and other personal items were returned. The only thing missing was the money. I guess they forgot to return it along with everything else. Mom had always been known as a go-getter, the kind of woman that gets things done. But after this incident, she earned the reputation of "Tenacious Tornado Mom from Texas." I wonder if that was why some people started calling me "The Twisted Twister?" Is it really possible that I was actually becoming more like my mother? Or were they just talking about my driving again?

My sisters and I used to spend long, hot, lazy summers on my grandparents' ranch in Texas as kids. Those sweet, summer moments were marked by a house full of family, friends, horseback riding, swimming, playhouses, incredible, starry nights, and lots of laughter. My grandmother raised Shetland ponies and spent many fulfilling years acquiring ponies of championship bloodlines, as well as a few old hags who managed to wrap their reigns around her heart. Naturally, after grandma passed away, some of her favorites endeared themselves to our hearts too. One old mare named Ruby bonded hard and fast to my sisters. Ruby was small in stature, even for a Shetland, but she seated a six and seven-year-old very nicely.

My grandparents built a wonderful two-story brick home that was perfect for hide-and-go-seek and ghost storytelling, but as in most houses that were built in the 1930s, there was no ramp. The need to build one became very apparent soon after I got my first Everest & Jennings electric wheelchair.

Jumping five concrete steps just to get in and out of the house seemed a bit outrageous even for an "Evil Kinevel wanna be." Both of my parents have wonderfully dry senses of humor, but dad is infamously known for his spontaneous silliness. We had no clue that when my father had the "Rube Goldberg-blue light special" ramp complete with the rubber non-slick surface built for the back door, he would use it to do a reenactment of Noah's ark, with a twist.

On a leisurely July morning, mom was drinking coffee at the breakfast table with our "southern bell, Scarlet O'Hara" cousin, Ella Mae from Atlanta, who had striking red hair and gorgeous marble brown eyes. Dad always enjoyed shocking her, so he decided to pull one of his unique stunts to turn her visit into something she would never forget. He succeeded in accomplishing what he set out to do. Mom and Ella Mae were deep in riveting conversation when all of a sudden, they were interrupted by the sound of hooves on a hard surface. Christmas was more than six months away so the possibility of reindeer on the roof was quickly ruled out.

Even though my interpretation is a bit on the far side, in the same way Noah loaded the animals onto the ark two by two, my two little chipmunk-cheeked sisters entered the kitchen in similar fashion—except they were on a horse, (Remember Ruby, the Shetland pony?) and dad was the proverbial "Noah" boisterously singing his favorite Gene Autry song, *We're back in the saddle again*. Mom, being the proper lady she is, never said a foul word, even though dad had turned her kitchen into a temporary horse stable. Audrey Hepburn had nothing on her. Instead of getting irate as most people would have about seeing a horse in the house, she simply looked at my dad and said something to the tune of, "Oh, my lord, James, what in the world do you think you're doing? We've discussed this before. This is not a ride-in restaurant such as Sonic or Mr. Burger!"

After the initial shock of having a live horse in our kitchen, things somewhat quieted down enough for someone to grab a camera and record the spectacle. The blockbuster movie *Grease* had just become a number one hit and had quite an influence on my young personal assistant Jewels and me. Jewels was a wonderful source of entertainment for my sisters and me. The 5'2" blue-eyed drama queen was infamously known for her theatrical "breakouts." It was not unusual for her to hit the floor on a bent knee and break out in a song or a Shakespearean soliloquy. True to form, when Jewels saw Ruby and the girls posing for the photo shoot, she took the toothbrush that was already in one hand and tickled Ruby's nose with the other to make Ruby appear to be smiling. She exclaimed "Hey, Jonean, look!" and then sang the jingle from an old toothpaste commercial, "Brusha, brusha, brusha—" which also appeared in the movie *Grease*. After seeing it as many times as we did, it was no mystery that Jewels and I knew almost every line by heart. As you can imagine, that jingle made a lasting impression on everyone in the room that day, including an old run-down hag of a horse.

Ruby had been an extraordinarily gracious sport about this escapade until around the time when she decided that she'd had enough and proceeded to lead *herself* out of the kitchen door. One might say this is where the rubber hit the road, or more applicable, where the hooves hit the linoleum. Dad had no idea that poor old Ruby had zero traction on linoleum. It looked as if mom and Jewels were lining up for a giant balloon toss while dad was desperately trying to help Ruby by holding her back end up and gingerly guiding her out of the door. Both my sisters and Ruby were caught in mid-air. But don't worry, no children or animals were damaged during the production of this practical joke. Needless to say, it was an extremely memorable visit for our cousin.

I would be remiss if I did not at least mention the infamous drive-thru crash. As many young people do, I went through a *cruisin'* stage. Jewels and I eagerly awaited the times when my parents sent us to town on errands or just to get us out of their hair. Many times, the only car that was available for us to drive was my grandmother's 1966 white Cadillac. It was in mint condition. The key word is, *was*. We were both so short that we looked like two, little old low-rider ladies dragging Main Street, but we felt as cool as hot chilies in an extra value burrito. After our usual order at the Sonic drive-in, we made our way to the Kodak picture hut to pick up some film for mom. When I say hut, that's exactly what I mean. It was basically four pieces of plywood nailed together with a flimsy roof that had a Kodak sign on the top. "Tornado targets" such as these were made purely for customer convenience, not durability.

For you who are unfamiliar with the classic 1966 Cadillacs, they were beautiful but also a nightmare to park horizontally. This is especially true for the vertically challenged people who have trouble seeing over the dashboard. Short legs and short arms go together, and Jewels fit that description to a tee. She drove up beside the hut as close as she could to reach the drop-off window. Everything was rolling along nicely until we started to pull away with more than we purchased. The back handle of the car somehow became attached to the front of the hut and we proceeded to uproot it from its original spot and take it with us. After the initial shock of surviving a "drive-by swipe" with no bodily harm, the poor clerk was very understanding, considering the fact that we'd just endangered her life. She also had a great sense of humor, evidenced by what she said afterwards: "Young ladies, can't you tell the difference between a drive-thru and a drive-in?"

The short drive home became a long, hot, tortuous one as an even more dreaded arrival awaited us. No amount of rehearsing could prepare us for the disquieting task of telling my parents that the family heirloom car was no longer in mint condition. So, we did the only thing that made sense. We cried and begged for mercy! After breaking the news, we all filed out of the back door to assess the damage. We walked to the car with our heads hung low, resembling a very short funeral procession on a hot, summer day. Jewels and I wondered if we were not indeed headed to our own burial plot. Those brief moments we watched my dad slowly inspect the car felt like hours of agony. Talk about two nervous ninnies who were "waiting to exhale." Dad finally broke the deafening silence.

"Jewels, been driving long?"

* * *

After those crazy, lazy days of summer were over, it was time once again to gear up for another school year. I was a bit hesitant when my cousin suddenly came up with a "perfect" assistant for me. I mentally ran through a checklist of all the pranks I pulled on her over the years. When I couldn't come up with anything too dastardly, I assumed that her recommendation was not an act of retribution. In fact, it was an act of great kindness.

My parents were still desperately seeking a Mary Poppins type of assistant with hopes of keeping me in line. Mom was beyond thrilled to find out Tricia came from a large, devout Catholic family. She had high hopes of finding someone like the character, Maria, in *The Sound of Music*. It makes me wonder if mom just secretly wanted Julie Andrews to be my personal assistant, since she had the leading role in both of those classic movies. Anyway, Tricia's aspiration to be a nun had passed early on in her youth. Many times she jokingly said that her desire to live in a convent was quenched after living with us. Tricia was constantly amazed because our household was the only place she knew of where one could get in trouble for saying the words, "gee whiz." Our parents considered those words to be only a step from the big "jeez" word which might eventually lead to uttering "Jesus" in a not so reverent manner. Though the logic may have been a bit on the far side, cussing or anything close to it was just not an option in our devout home.

The morning we finally met, I kept thinking that if this had been a date, at least we could have gone very separate ways after struggling through a few hours of boring chitchat. But, since Tricia was willing to fly across states from Oklahoma to California to make a trial run with me, I figured I needed to attempt more than just polite conversation. As I reluctantly wheeled into the living room, I saw that she was comfortably seated in front of the plate glass window, looking out over the Pacific Ocean with a calm but pensive look in her translucent hazel eyes. Her long brown hair was cascading off her shoulders and down the back of the overstuffed armchair. It was a relief when those first few hours of conversation came so easily and soon turned into long, late night rap sessions. Tricia's personality was a magical combination of Annie Sullivan and Stevie Nicks. Her gentle nature made it easy to become close friends.

Tricia rarely got mad but when she did, she would simply

leave for a while to cool off. At times this felt worse than being yelled at or slapped. Her eyes always reflected a peaceful look that reminded me of the saying, "still waters run deep." When she was upset, those waters indicated a definite stirring underneath. One of my funniest memories of Tricia that exemplifies this was the night we babysat my sisters. Bedtime had come and, as usual, they exercised their right to protest. Tricia gazed at them with a look that said she had heard all the flack that she could handle about going to bed. She very calmly walked into the bathroom, locked the door behind her, and stayed in there for about an hour. After proving that beating on the door and screaming was not going to make her come out, both of my sisters began to worry. They sat very quietly by the door until she gingerly opened it. They took one look at her face, and made a run for their beds without another sound.

I admired the way Tricia handled tense situations, but I felt bad that she missed out on being at home when her first niece was born because she was attending to me. She came from a large, tight-knit family that enjoyed turning any event into a reason to get together. So you can imagine the remorse I felt watching her cry as she listened to her brother describe how awesome the birth was and how beautiful the baby was. I anxiously wheeled around the house trying to find a box of Kleenex. There was no doubt this was serious because not even a big piece of mom's chocolate cake could console her this time. She went down to her room early that night without saying a word.

Does the cliché "paranoia will destroy ya" ring any bells for you? They sure were ringing loudly for me that night. What did Tricia mean by not saying good night? Would I still have a personal assistant, or would she make her great escape and disappear into the night? After an hour of entertaining these thoughts, I rode the elevator down to the first floor, racking my brain trying to think of something clever to say that would lighten her mood and somehow make it seem worth her while to stick around a little longer. My experience with different personal assistants up to this point had heightened my awareness of special people that I wanted to hang on to, and those who I wished would find somewhere else to hang. Tricia was definitely worth trying to hang on to.

As I apprehensively opened the heavy elevator door, it suddenly occurred to me to make this occasion a celebration rather than an interrogation to try and figure out her plans. After all, I had seen people open bottles of champagne or wine to celebrate a child's birth. I was hoping this would make her niece's birthday a very memorable date in more ways than one. Surely my parents wouldn't miss one bottle from their wine collection if I got it from the back. At least that was what I was hoping. After successfully picking up a bottle without dropping it on the tile floor, which was quite a feat considering how shaky I was from both nervousness and spasticity, I made my way to Tricia's room. Living with the type of cerebral palsy that I have makes simple movements such as extending an arm feel like a small battle of tug-of-war with both one's self and gravity. I'm convinced God has a wonderful sense of humor because He answers bizarre prayer requests like, "Oh God, please let me get this bottle on my lap so that my parents won't ask me what was spilled on the floor." If caught, confessing to a missing bottle did not seem nearly as bad as confessing to an empty one and a big mess on the floor. My parents are very neat people and strongly disapprove of alcohol consumption under the age of thirty. At the time I was seventeen, and getting caught would have led to punishment for the next eight years! Being suave was risky business but I was going to do it. As I looked into Tricia's puffy eyes, I cheerfully asked if she would like a drink to celebrate her niece's arrival.

The conversation began with Tricia asking, "What ya doing"?

I responded: "Thought you might like a drink to celebrate Abby's birthday."

With a raised eyebrow, Tricia inquired further.

"Where did that come from and how in the world did you get it?"

"The grape fairy got it very carefully from mom and dad's collection," I sheepishly replied.

Now, Tricia's voice along with both of her eyebrows were raised.

"And do they know you have it"?

"Not exactly, but they won't mind. They're so happy

about Abby, you know."

"Are you sure about that? It doesn't sound like your mom would find it quite kosher," she said.

"Oh, sure, they won't care," I said, trying to sound cool and collected.

After considerable coercion, Tricia agreed that a drink would be nice. She poured herself a glass, and a half glass for me. It tasted like a lemon wrapped in dirty socks, but I did everything I could not to make a face. She saw the tears in my eyes from the nasty taste in my mouth and said, "Please tell me you've drunk before."

"Of course," I said, "Yes, oh yes, I've tasted some before. Isn't this good?"

That half glass was all it took to prove that this was indeed a first for me. Who knew that such a small glass of wine could loosen my lips so much? I would not shut up! Poor Tricia ended up being amazed instead of consoled that night. I asked her every question except for the one I really wanted to know: was she staying or going?

The next morning, I woke up thinking, if she leaves, it won't be to move closer to her niece. It'll be to get away from me—the "suave" conversationalist in a wheelchair. As the night wrapped up, Tricia made a smart move and told me that she was tired and wanted to turn in. I was kind of tired, too, so I drove my wheelchair to the elevator just as I had done a hundred times before. Tricia opened the heavy elevator door for me to back into it. I turned around and started to back up. Boom! I hit the wall. I smiled and tried again.

Bang! I hit the side of the door. I was embarrassed but I said, "Let's try this again." Crash! My chair hit the edge of the elevator so hard it spun sideways. "Oops! One more time."

Ten minutes and many tries later, we were both laughing hysterically. Tricia saw the hopelessness of the situation, took control, and wheeled me safely into the elevator. When she could finally close the door with all my limbs inside, she grinned and asked, "So, how long have you been driving?"

On the elevator ride back to my room, my laughter subsided as I came to the realization that I needed to get out quickly and quietly because my little sisters were already in bed. Furthermore, mom would have killed me twice over if she found out what I had been doing downstairs when I was supposed to be upstairs fast asleep. DING! The elevator stopped. I quietly pulled back the gate and tried to open the heavy door. The harder I pushed, the louder the elevator floor squeaked and rattled. My chair was doing the side-ways shuffle as I tried with all my might to escape what was starting to feel like a hell hole. Just as I backed up to make one more run for the door, I heard footsteps shuffling on the thick shag rug. The theme song from the movie "Jaws" quickly crescendoed in my head. I tried to be as quiet as a mouse in hopes that whoever it was would ignore the commotion and keep walking by, but the handle turned, and the heavy door jerked open. There was no doubt about it now. I had been found out. I felt like the Cheshire Cat from *Alice in Wonderland* caught in a mousetrap. I took a few short breaths, anticipating the full weight of my parent's wrath. What can one say in a moment such as this, except "Hi," followed by a megawatt smile. The door opened and I was face to face with dear ol' dad standing there, trying to figure out the cause of all the ruckus. If there was anything he'd learned with three creative daughters, it was this: some things are better left unsaid, or in my case, unasked. He took one look at me and said, in his deep, sarcastic voice, "You been driving long?"

Chapter 2
1982-1984

Well, excuse me, but I think you've got my chair!

Tricia decided she had experienced all the adolescent fun she could handle and left to be closer to her family the day after I graduated. My high school graduation was the first time in my life that I realized it was possible to look forward to an event with all of my heart and soul, yet dread it with the same intensity. Taking into consideration that the doctor's prognosis for me at six months of age was a little above a head of lettuce, graduation was not only a milestone in my life, but also in my parents' lives. Nearly my entire family came to celebrate this "modern day miracle." We had all been looking forward to that day with great anticipation but knowing that Tricia was moving 3,000 miles away the next day made me wish my heart was made of stone.

The older I get, the more I'm convinced that the nitty-gritty, everyday tasks, combined with the crazy emotional roller coaster times in our lives are the "ups and downs" of the abundant life that Christ has in mind for all of us. He grants us opportunities to experience all sorts of extremes so that we can truly know the abundance of a full life. We may feel totally undeserving or inadequate to handle everything that comes our way, but He always provides the tools for us to go through situations and learn from them. It may not always be obvious why overwhelming situations come our way, but from experience, I know some of the most surprising joys in life come disguised in the most unattractive packages. After living so closely with Tricia for two years, it was very hard to imagine not having her to pal around with or share all of my secrets with. She had become much more than just a friend or an employee. Tricia was the big sister I had always hoped for. She was the one who participated in my arbitrary shenanigans that etched long-lasting, happy memories in my mind. Take, for instance, the time she covered for me while I went to a cast party and rode around with Hugh, the guy who was the object of my first real crush. My parents would not have approved of me being in close contact with any guy without a "responsible third wheel." I cleverly avoided the issue of my curfew by spending the night at my best friend Necie's house. I felt reasonably safe because even if my parents had seen me riding around with this handsome, talented cellist, I knew Necie could charm the socks off an angel with her Aussie accent and huge hazel eyes. She could talk her way out of anything!

As for my crush, nothing ever came of it. I suspected it was because he had his own little crush on the beautiful redhead in our class. He always did have good taste. Then there were the times we would periodically rush into class before anyone else got there and trade places. Tricia would put me into one of the desk chairs and she would sit in my wheelchair. Then we would sit back to see how many double or triple takes we could get. We found it very amusing that the teachers always seemed to be taken off guard by this child-like trickery, while my peers appeared to be thinking, "get some new material."

When I went back for my twenty-year reunion, a few of my peers had that same confused expression on their faces. It's funny how some things never change. Although no irreparable damage was ever done on these little jaunts of self-discovery and fun, Tricia wanted out of the risky business of watching me provoke my parents' wrath. She thought if my high school yearnings were any indication of things to come, she would gladly take her exit.

As with most first born children, I seemed to always have had the gift of flabbergasting my parents. Not only was it an unspoken expectation that they wanted me to be perfect because of the love and one-on-one attention lavished upon me as the first child, but it stood to reason that as severe as my disability is, I would have little choice but to be on my best behavior at all times. I think this was why it was so hard on them when I made one of many senseless "declarations of independence." I was a rebel without a cause because it was trendy. Even though Tricia was an innocent bystander in most cases, she would be sentenced as guilty by association in whatever mischief I cooked up if we were caught. Some of my favorite assistants have claimed that one of the most difficult tasks that came along with the job was walking the thin, fiery line between my parent's expectations, and the goofy, fun things that rocked my world. Like that one day during the spring semester of my senior year. It's a day that'll go down in infamy.

This was one of the very few times when Tricia was an accomplice to the crime, because she was the one able to drive the getaway car. Now is a good time to tell you that during my senior year, I had the privilege of being the first student with any type of major disability to grace the campus of Carmel High School. As with any first honor, there are certain advantages and disadvantages. One of the advantages was that the "Adaptive" Physical Education program was non-existent at Carmel High in that era. This was a definite perk because I'd experienced so many physical therapy programs by this time, I developed a gag reflex at the sight of an exercise mat. It was announced that an adaptive P.E. instructor, Miss Jasmine, had joined the staff at the onset of my senior year. The school board's decision to make this course a new requirement for graduation "just for my benefit" could not have come at a worse time, considering the hormonal hell I was already going through. I could not believe the nerve of the school asking me to stay an extra class period while the other seniors were dismissed at noon! This meant that I would have to forfeit a trip to the ice cream parlor and miss out on at least an hour and a half of sunbathing at the beach. I should have gotten a degree in whining and dining because I excelled in both by that point in my life.

The P.E. instructor truly made an effort to make amends for this injustice by making each Friday a "senior skip day" if I attended class the other four days. It was too much for me. I skipped not just Fridays, but all the other days too. My pattern was to hit and miss class on Tuesdays or Wednesdays, depending on the weather and my mood. Believe it or not, I eventually became reasonably good friends with Jasmine towards the end of the year, although our friendship didn't begin until a humbling attitude adjustment. We've all probably heard that God works in mysterious and wonderful ways. On a particularly warm Thursday in early spring during my senior year, God intervened in a mysterious, but not exactly wonderful, way.

My day started out just as every other day did with me, anxiously awaiting lunch but dreading P.E. afterwards. Since Carmel High did not have a traditional dine-in cafeteria at that time, Tricia and I would eat in or on my car while listening to some tunes and getting a bit of sun. If friends wanted to join us at our little "blacktop escape," they knew where to come. By this time, our group included Jasmine. It became a habit for her to cheerfully stop by our car under the guise of a casual greeting, but I knew she was checking to see if I was sticking around for class. It just so happened that of the three and a half years I'd been in high school, my mom chose this beautiful, sunny, beach weather day to grace us with her presence for lunch. When I saw her smiling face as we approached the car, all I could think was, "Thank goodness we decided to stay through lunch today." I can't deny that it was kind of cool, but odd to see my elegant mother eating lunch with us out of the back of my baby blue Datsun 210 hatchback station wagon, talking to my friends as they passed by. As we critiqued the classic 80's fashion statements walking by, up walks my statuesque, ballerina shaped, "let's get physical" P.E. instructor with her leotard top and wool leggings. The lump in my throat grew as I realized all the unpleasant but colorful facts she could share with mom. Out of the corner of my eye, 1 saw Tricia quietly chuckling at the familiar deer in the headlights look on my face. Knowing how friendly Jasmine was, I knew there was no way out of this awkward moment. I wanted to twitch my nose (as they did in *Bewitched*) and vanish, but all I could do was smile big and introduce mom to Jasmine. I was very relieved to witness their conversation flowing pleasantly, but still waiting hopefully for her to go on to class without explaining to mom why I wouldn't be receiving the perfect attendance award for the year.

Just as I thought I was going to be saved by the bell,

Jasmine nonchalantly said as she walked away, "Oh Jonean, so glad you could make it today. We sure missed you yesterday!" I politely thanked her and gave mom my best Lucille Ball look knowing I had a lot of explaining to do! As luck would have it, mom never said a word about it. She just gave me a chastising look. That's all it took for me to get my act together.

After a month of begging Tricia to stay after graduation, until I adapted to an independent lifestyle, she left in June. Even though I could hardly wait to taste, touch, and feel the co-ed life away from the overprotective supervision of my parents, I was very apprehensive to experience it without the watchful eyes of Tricia. She claimed that keeping me out of trouble with my parents was challenging enough during the last two years of high school, so she was glad to pass on the experimental days of college. Once again we were faced with the nerve-racking experience of finding "the right one." This time, it took almost eight months for the dependable ad to work its charm.

Nerve-racking hardly does justice in describing this insane period of my life—especially for my parents. I started school in August at a junior college with mom's help. That experience alone is enough for a whole other book. Dad stayed with my sisters and tried to keep the home fires burning. Mom had to come to the rescue once more because the personal assistant that started the semester with me got cold feet by the third week and quit. It did not do much for my ego or my sense of security when she forgot her way back after her first weekend home. My whole family pitched in and not only made it possible for me to finish that fall semester, but also made some unforgettable memories.

As the fall leaves turned and blew by, the seasonal witches began to gather. Halloween was always a favorite, festive event at our house. Since we seemed to live on the outskirts of town, we did not have the luxury of trick-or-treating in our own neighborhood. To make up for this childhood tragedy, mom or dad would answer the front door while we circled our house several times with our poor, confused dog. When my sisters saw that I was now living in a neighborhood where they could actually go trick-or-treating, they jumped on it like a witch on her broom. By this time, my sweet, spunky, little eighty-year old grandma had come to lend mom and I a hand, and to fatten us up with her heavenly cooking. I come from a house full of wannabe comedians. My grandma was no exception. In fact, she gave us all a run for our money when it came to the art of tomfoolery. This particular Halloween proved no different.

When the trick-or-treaters were no longer bombarding our door, along came a tall, lanky straggler. Mom was hesitant about opening the door because it obviously wasn't a kid. But what was it? The six-foot plus he/she was adorned with a heavy, wool stocking cap, a long, old-fashioned, off-white "house coat," brown pants, purple socks, penny loafers, and a pair of dark knee-highs on his/her head and face. Mom partly opened the door in case she was grabbed and needed to slam it quickly on a body part. She gingerly put a few pieces of candy in the out- stretched brown paper bag. In a wee voice that sounded like the haunting voice of the psychotic girl from the movie, "Don't Say A Word," we heard, "thank you." But instead of taking the candy and running off like everyone else, this person just kept standing in the doorway. This intensely scary moment enticed all of us to take a closer look. It was almost surreal. The person looked at us as if we should have known who they were. In retrospect, the purple socks and ridiculous loafers should have been a dead giveaway (no pun intended) to the identity of this mystery person. In the midst of the chaos we didn't realize that grandma had mysteriously disappeared. To this day, I don't know how she snuck right past the three of us on the way to the garage, but she did! For the first time in my life, I was glad that mom had a deep yearning to be a member of the *paparazzi*. She made sure that all the monumental events of our lives were recorded, no matter how embarrassing. Her large Minolta camera with the super zoom lens was always close at hand, giving her full access to our finer moments. Photographing my grandma in that get up was better than what American Express claims to be. Priceless.

It was after Christmas break when my next victim, Meg, answered the ad. By that time, I had passed the first semester of school with somewhat flying colors and was ready to have some fun experiencing the college life that I had heard about.

No offense to my mom, but she had a special way of focusing my attention on academic activities instead of extracurricular ones. Meg had raised her family and was looking for a new start. She was ready to have some fun, too. So, what do you think we did? We had some fun! Our household was known for spontaneous combustion. The neighbors were often entertained by the whimsical activities that we became notorious for. Even our front yard reflected our distinctive personalities. We were there for about eight months when our neighbors began asking if Tarzan had moved in. Three nice, able-bodied people informed me that they would be happy to mow my lawn. I politely declined and took matters into my own "wheels" instead. Since my chair was equipped with a power pack battery on the back, all I needed was a push-mower to have a power mower. So on a bright, sunny Saturday morning, I set out to tame the jungle. When I asked Meg to pry out the dinky push-mower that was crammed behind a stack of boxes, she gave me an indignant look as if to say, "I don't do lawns on the weekends!" But that look turned into uncontrollable laughter when I informed her of my plan to mow the lawn myself. Her attitude made me even more determined to successfully accomplish this domesticated home-owner's task. It felt like sweet justice when she had to hobble inside to prevent a bladder blow-out from laughing so hard. By the time I finished "motoring" that dinky mower between my legs, my slightly overgrown yard looked as if it had survived a bad punk haircut. The choppy look may work as a hairstyle, but it made my lawn look like a crime scene. By the time I finished there were long patches of grass here, there and everywhere. It looked like a crooked mohawk on a balding guy suffering from mange. Too bad I couldn't charge for the looks I received from my neighbors. I could have paid tuition for a semester in college. Two things I can confidently say. The "Joneses" *never* tried to keep up with this neighbor, and I never again had to worry about mowing my yard. Someone always seemed to magically mow the lawn before I got to it. Never underestimate the power of independence.

Another situation that made the neighbors shake their heads and deny knowing us came one day after class when Meg spotted a pair of roller skates in our garage that belonged to a friend's daughter. I dared her to put them on and race around the block. True to her character, Meg could hardly stand to pass up a dare, especially if it came from yours truly. It took a bit of finagling to get her Annie Oakley two-toned boots off and squeeze her tired, sweaty feet into those lace-up roller skates, but she refused to give in to the agony of "de feet." As you can imagine, we caught the eyes of a few spectators as we whirled through the neighborhood. Things were rolling right along until we started up a rather steep slope. Suddenly, the lead that Meg had on my old Everest & Jennings electric wheelchair quickly diminished and I was "getting jiggy with it." Even though Meg will always claim that my lead was a technicality, I won because my footrests were clearly ahead of her. I screamed for victory when we were neck in neck. Just as my back tires prepared to leave her in the dust, Meg grabbed the handles on the back of my chair and held on for dear life. With a certain southern charm and grace, the classic cowpoke song, "Happy Trails" bellowed out of her mouth. As we were coming in for our final approach, my footrests bouncing off the incline of our driveway, the long-awaited cable guy came into view. He had unfortunately shown up on time, and was watching the show we had unwittingly put on with great enjoyment. Meg and I sheepishly grinned and tried to avoid eye contact as we whizzed past and entered the house. Maybe I thought that if we sped through the door, the poor man would forget the ridiculous sight he had just beheld, or I was hoping he would be so befuddled by it that he wouldn't ask questions. I hoped in vain. After he finished, he looked straight at me and asked, "So, are we having some fun with mom today?" Knowing full well that my mother would never be caught dead making such a goofy spectacle of herself and taking the chance that he would probably never actually meet mom, I decided to lie. I mean, what's the harm in a little white lie? I did what any mature twenty-year old would do. I promptly said, "yes, sir," then quickly wheeled away, and let Meg do all of the explaining!

Even though this time in my life seemed to be filled with spontaneous fun and games, there were occasions when it was a very good thing there were no guns in our household. I suppose if we had allowed firearms in our humble abode, we could've called it the house of "guns and roses!" Two strong-willed women living under the same roof made homicide seem justifiable at times. This next adventure is an example.

Meg and I became good friends with two, nice, young couples who were also making their way through school. All of us had one dangerous love in common. Practical jokes. We loved to prank others, and ourselves. As my luck would have it, my neighbors were masterminds who could blow me out of the water any day. Kendal was studying to become a veterinarian and was always explaining my behavior in animal terms. His fiancée Rachel was a beautiful red-headed chemistry major. It is entirely due to her brains and patience that I passed Algebra and Chemistry. Kailey was our Italian blonde bombshell who was the daredevil of the group. She was always off to scuba diving lessons or equestrian lessons and tried to get everyone else to join in. She worked as hard as she played. Her boyfriend Alex was the quiet one of the group but when he spoke, everyone listened. He had already graduated and was a pilot for a local airline.

My wits were on overload each time we all got together. To give you an idea of the pranksters I was up against, one semester they all decided it would be a nice gesture to take me to breakfast at a truck stop. The only problem was that everyone neglected to inform me of the devilish plan. They said it was a "kidnap breakfast," which was a problem because I often slept in little less than my skivvies! Not that Meg deserves it, but I must give credit where credit is due. She did try to warn me in her own little odd way. She informed me it was supposed to get cold that night and said I might consider wearing pajamas. With my usual attitude at that time, I considered her suggestion another silly attempt to control me since it was over ninety degrees that day. But when my lamp flipped on at 5:30 a.m. and out of my squinted, sleep-filled eyes, I beheld Rachel, Kailey, and Meg staring at me like three monkeys, her bizarre advice did not seem so silly after all! With some righteous indignation, knowing full well that I was not nor would I ever be a morning person, I could not fathom what these people were doing in my room at that hour. One good look at each of their smiling faces and it was totally under the covers for me. They taunted me with the old line, "Come out, come out, however you are!" My pleas, threats and bribes, fell on deaf ears. They were not going away. I gravely realized that they were going to play dirty when they called for backup in the next room. Kendal and Alex were waiting for the sign to come in to manhandle me out of bed. They did not have to wait long because the girls could see that I had absolutely no intentions of budging. The "goons" came to the foot of my bed and were waiting with bated breath for a sign to pull back the covers. That was enough to convince me to surrender and beg for Meg's help. Though she was laughing all the way, Meg finally came to her senses and conducted damage control before the guys got too "helpful" by getting me to promise to get up if they would step out. Although she succeeded in getting them out of my room, the girls were another story. But I would almost bet my life that Rach and Kailey never pulled that stunt again. The shock of seeing me come out of that bed in all my glory was almost enough to pay them back for waking me up at that ungodly hour. After witnessing the shape that I was in, they finally conceded to "allow" me to wear a flimsy ensemble of a white and blue striped robe complete with high top sneakers to the fancy 24-hour truck stop. I guess as gorgeous as I looked, they wouldn't risk taking me to Denny's. After all, their reputations were on the line.

It must have appeared as though these "nice people" were taking this poor, sick woman in a robe and sneakers out on a day pass as we unloaded out of my trusty hatch-back. At first, I was grateful that the young waitress escorted us to a back corner booth. Then, I realized that this only gave the truckers a more up close and personal view of my latest fashion statement. Don't worry, I kept my big sunglasses on just in case anyone recognized me. As we passed tables and booths, I couldn't help but wonder if *this* was the reason for mom's insistence on always wearing a clean robe and underwear!

During that year of payback for payback, Kendal and Rachel tied the knot. Their picture-perfect wedding was held near Los Angeles where my godparents lived, so Meg and I thought we would make it an extra-long weekend and stay with them after the wedding. As time ticked closer and closer to the big day, the summer session was ending, and I couldn't wait to get out of dodge. Since I had a strong "B" in psychology, I skipped the review for the final and left a day early. The saying, "God takes care of fools and babies" is very true. Practicality was not my strong point at the time, and Meg was not the type to hold me back. She essentially gave me the freedom to fall on my face, then helped me up while hysterically laughing. A lot of my adventures resembled Lucy and Ethel moments straight out of a television episode. This trip was no exception.

Since I was going to miss all the festivities the night before the big wedding, I felt it was only right to take the bride for one last single girls' night out. Rachel and I went to one of our favorite little beer gardens by the river that flowed through the middle of San Luis Obispo. It was a charming place where local bands would play on the weekends. One could lose all sense of time listening to great music, taking in the smells, sights, and reflections of trees swaying on the water. This evening was no different. I indeed lost all track of time but not in the way that you're probably thinking. As I said before, Rachel could have been a model. She was a tall, classic, red head with alabaster skin and the kind of oceanic, blue eyes that guys dive into and have trouble coming up from for air. There has always been something fascinating to me about girls like her, who could strike the perfect balance between beauty and down-home charm. She kept a tin of chewing tobacco in her back pocket. I mention it only because the skill of spitting tobacco has also always interested me. My grandfather was an avid chewer, but it always seemed paradoxical to see a beautiful woman with a stream of tobacco spewing from her lips. By now you know me well enough to predict that I couldn't leave it alone, but this time curiosity almost did indeed kill the cat (me-ouch).

After dinner, Rach popped out her can and delicately grabbed a pinch of dark brown tobacco and stuck it deep inside her bottom lip. I hate to admit it, but I was watching and unconsciously imitating the movement of her mouth opening to receive it as somebody opens their own mouth when they are trying to feed a baby. She embarrassingly admitted that Kendal was the one who got her started "chewing." She continued because it gave her a nice boost any time of day. I'm not promoting the use of tobacco, but apparently Kendal had "all the right snuff!" I couldn't stand it any longer and I asked if she could spare a pinch. She hesitated and asked if I was sure. And of course, I proclaimed, "Oh, yes, I've always wondered what it tastes like." I can only think of one word to describe this stomach-churning experience—DISGUSTING!

Working hard to keep up my cosmopolitan image, I tried not to cringe while simultaneously saying, "Wow!" I normally don't have any problem with drooling. In fact, I'm quite good at this activity. But on this particular evening, I found drooling exceedingly gross and disgusting. So, I swallowed it, and then it hit me like a punch once I realized how terrible of a mistake I'd just made. The ten-minute drive on the freeway to my house felt like a thirty-minute roller coaster ride on

Space Mountain at Disneyland. I was like one of Rachel's photosynthesis projects gone askew. I turned greener with every passing mile. By the time we hit the driveway and headed into the garage, it was time. Rachel helped me out of the car and into my chair as she tried not to bust a gut laughing! Meg had stepped into the garage with the suitcases she had packed while we were gone. As you can imagine, her greeting was not what you would call overly welcoming. She took one look at the situation as I was slowly sliding out of my chair and asked what the heck happened. Though the incriminating evidence looked much worse than the crime, we both tried to tell the story as gently as possible. Rach started and finished because before the first word formed in my mouth, my head started spinning like the little girl's in *The Exorcist*. Although the words had trouble coming out, the nice dinner we had did not. It flowed like Old Faithful in Yellowstone National Park. The next thing I remember was waking up in my bed, wondering why we hadn't left for the wedding yet. I guess you can say I gave Rachel a spewing send off!

You would think since Meg and I were already off to a rough start, and short on cash, we would have waited to leave a little later. But we didn't. We left a day early, eager to hit the road. As on any good road trip, we snacked and talked so much about food that we worked up a ferocious appetite. Pooling our funds together and scrounging for loose change on the floorboard, we found enough money to either have a nice meal or stay at the hotel where we had reservations the next night. I convinced Meg that we should try to find this famous Polynesian restaurant where movie stars supposedly hung out and worry about lodging later. Amazingly, she listened to me. It would be nice, after all, to see some real stars other than the ones Meg kept threatening to show me if I ever dipped tobacco again. So off we went, following bad directions, listening to the car horns of angry drivers as we drove the wrong way on a one-way street. After all that, I sure hoped the food would be worth the trouble it took us to find this place. But, by this point our hunger pangs were so strong, anything but roadkill would have been tasty. We finally arrived, and the food was totally worth us wandering in the wilderness for two and half-hours.

As our stomachs slowly filled and our moods lightened, it became safer to discuss our accommodations for the night. Since we knew the hotel where we had reservations was in the same vicinity as the wedding activities, we decided to drive in that direction. Don't ask me why it didn't occur to either of us to look for a cheaper room nearby. I guess our logic was that it was already late, we could check in early where we had reservations the next morning, so why waste money? We parked in front of the hotel door in a well-lit area and slept until check-in time. The back seats folded down so we used our beach blankets for padding. Neither one of us are extremely tall, so by putting the luggage in the front floorboard we made just enough room to lie down in the back. Everything seemed to fit inside the car except for my wheelchair. It was an older model with a bulky metal frame and spokes. Unfortunately, it did not fold up as easily or as compactly as the newer models do now. So, to allow more space to stretch out, we left my chair outside by the passenger door. It seemed like the practical thing to do. I had finally reached the edge of the twilight zone when I thought I heard the wheels on my chair begin slowly squeaking away. I brushed it off as the tired wheels in my head that refused to stop spinning. The squeaking became increasingly louder the harder I tried to silence the noise in my mind. I opened one eye and vaguely saw figures moving through the mist on the windows.

"Meg!" I shouted, "Wake up! There are some people out there."

"Yeah, 'course there are. It's a great big world," she answered.

"No, Meg, I mean it. They are out there, and they've got my chair. Come on, wake up!"

By this time, I was panicking. If some dimwits had stolen my chair, I was up a creek and stuck in the middle. There would be no way to attend the wedding or visit my godparents without it; not to mention the dreadful task of explaining to my parents where and how my chair was stolen.

"Meg, wake up now!" I exclaimed.

Meg exhaustedly raised her head and opened one eye and said, "Okay, okay, I'm up. What did you say about your chair?"

"Just look outside. They have my wheelchair."

"Who?" Meg slurred out.

"Some UFOs. I don't know. How should I know?"

Meg wiped off a small portion of the window so she could see out and said, "Oh my, they're playing tag baseball with your chair!"

"What are we going to do about it?"

"We? You mean, what am *I* going to do about getting it back. With my luck, they're probably on something. Maybe they will just go away," she sarcastically added. It was a nice thought, but they did not go away. In fact, they were having such a good time running bases with my chair that they didn't notice we were watching them.

After some debate, we frantically came up with a game plan. We decided on the count of three Meg would burst out from the back door as dramatically as possible. I'm not sure if it was dramatic or traumatic, but she sure got the job done quickly. When she jumped out of the car, not only did she look like a jack-in-the-box wired to pounce on anything that moved, she also resembled one of those wild-eyed Spelunker trolls on the end of pencils. You know, those little dolls you spin, and the hair flies out of control? Upon witnessing her grand entrance, they were so astonished they were rendered speechless. In just seconds, those young people proved the adage "actions speak louder than words" really is true. Without hesitation, they readily gave the wheelchair back to us and ran for their lives into the night as she yelled after them, "Excuse me, but I think you've got my chair!"

Chapter 3
1984-1990

Getting stuck with Amanda, priceless!

After four years of abundant living, Meg and I decided we had experienced all the "Lucy and Ethel moments" we could handle. It was time to move on and go our separate ways. Although she had stayed much longer than the average assistant and endured the brunt of too many practical jokes that had long ceased to be funny, it was still hard for us to say goodbye. I had never spent four years so closely with anyone besides family. We shared many firsts in my life that greatly influenced the person I am today. There were two firsts during my time with Meg that will go down in my personal hall of fame. But first, if by some miracle, my fairy godmother came to me on a fluffy cloud of splendorous white and said I could change one thing about myself, there would be no need to contemplate. My speech impediment would win hands down. It wasn't until recently that I saw

God's wisdom in allowing me to have a speech impediment because in a few situations, I would probably already be experiencing life after death if some had understood me the first time.

Sometimes it is hard to tell if people truly have your best interest at heart have when they keep harping on changing your worst attribute. It is one thing for you to deal privately with your own demons, but quite another if these difficulties are noticeable enough for everyone to want to help you change. My "demon" was my embarrassment over my speech impediment. It wasn't until years later that I could take the "critic" out of constructive criticism and gain some of the most valuable knowledge I could have ever learned for free. But this revelation did not happen overnight. So, until I kind of grasped this concept, every time Meg made me color outside of the lines of my comfort zone, I became devastatingly defensive. This was especially true in regard to my speech. I felt I had already colored way outside of the lines by moving out on my own that year. It was the least that Meg could do to make this one area of my life easier. Although Meg and I were both incredibly grateful to have survived the road trip to Kendal and Rachel's big wedding with my wheelchair intact, murder appeared at the top of the to-do list soon after we arrived home. My way of thinking was: if Meg knew the sheer panic that came along each time I had to engage in any kind of interactive public speaking, she surely wouldn't have had the nerve to make me go retrieve a week's worth of mail our neighbors had collected while we were out of town. I would have much rather cleaned up backyard waste that had been collecting for three months from our dog than go and fetch the mail. Not that the task was beneath me, but Meg could get the mail much easier than I could. Besides that, she knew all too well that when I am tired, my articulation goes down the drain. We argued over who would go until all four of our eyeballs bugged out and there was hardly any more oxygen left in the room. My fate was sealed when Meg heard me say, "Well, it's a part of your job, not mine." Not too long after that, I found myself outside, wheeling very slowly to the neighbor's house with a list of my most concise, understandable phrases rolling through my head like credits at the end of a movie. I even contemplated how to say hello without sounding too mousy or forceful. Sometimes with cerebral palsy, one not only lacks valuable control of one's limbs but also breath control in stressful situations. Going through a few practice runs, I decided "hi" was the best choice.

With each turn of the wheels, their front door appeared closer and closer. Butterflies fluttered in my stomach so spastically, it's a wonder I didn't drive off the sidewalk! After I rang the neighbor's front doorbell, the temptation to quietly roll away and tell Meg they went out for pizza was irresistible. Just as I was about to make a "roll" for it, the squeaky deadbolt turned and there stood Mary with the most welcoming smile I had ever seen. There was definitely something about Mary that made me feel as if we had an instant bond. It was one of the most surprisingly refreshing experiences of that summer. The worst part of that lovely afternoon spent chatting about our goofy dogs over a cold one, Dr. Pepper that is, was going home to eat crow that Meg had especially prepared for me. Back in those days of many firsts, it seemed as if I had to constantly face dealing with my speech impediment. It was quite an ordeal if I got called on in class, even if I knew the correct answer. In high school, my English teachers sort of took pity on me when I humiliated myself by burping my way through a speech on the Canterbury Tales. Just the thought of that gastronomical nightmare could send me straight to bed. Imagine my terror when I discovered that Speech 101 was a requirement for graduation. Pure dread was only the tip of the iceberg of the range of emotions I felt before each speech. I begged, threatened, and pleaded with everyone I thought had the power to waive the class for me. They all had the same audacious reply, "I'm sorry, it's not possible to go against policy." Besides, "taking Speech will broaden your horizons." Thanks a lot, but I was very happy with my horizons which I thought were clearly broad enough.

As much as I truly hate to admit it, that speech class turned out to be one of the best undergraduate experiences I had. Our seasoned professor could not have chosen a better first assignment. It was the perfect ice breaker for a room full of "green around the gills" students. Our assignment was to give a speech on a hobby, or the process of an activity that we were passionate about. Since I did not have a real hobby back then, the professor let me do my speech on the obedience training of my nine-month-old Rottweiler puppy, Princess. I felt confident with the subject because we had just completed the second round of obedience classes with her and were seriously considering a third. Not that Princess was slow, but as any Rottweiler lover knows, they can be rather stubborn. After much rehearsing with and without Princess, I felt my speech, "Rott" rocked! I chose the second slot out of about ten students who were scheduled to make their spiel that night. That way, I would be spared the glare of the first spotlight but could avoid the probability of having a rather large, exuberant, puppy destroying the classroom.

Princess was bathed, walked and ready to show. I spent the afternoon getting in the zone, and ate a very light, early meal in order to ensure a burp-free speech. The first student to present was Sam aka "Marlboro Man" with his neatly trimmed mustache, and beautiful, ebony eyes. His speech was about the secret to making banana pancakes. Princess and I were prepared, but not for the temptation of banana pancakes fresh off the hotplate! My eye had been on the handsome Marlboro Man for some time now. We made small talk during the breaks but nothing really earth shaking. That is, until that day when I discovered Sam and Princess shared a special interest in the same hobby. Banana pancakes! I must admit, the smell coming from Sam's small hotplate was mouthwatering. It was obvious that Princess totally concurred from the streams of drool coming from her delicate, heavy jowls. Sam's great delivery held the audience captive right up until the end. Princess was so enthralled by his speech, she left me in my anxious state and went to beg for scraps. Traitor! Her sniffling could be heard all the way across the crowded room as well as the snickering that followed. In order to regain what little control I had of the situation, I asked Meg to take Princess outside while I got settled at the podium. I wanted to take her out myself but feared I wouldn't have come back.

The speech got off to a strong start. Princess posed regally as I told of the origin of her breed. Knowing that this stance would not last long, I tried to rush through it in hopes that Princess would not show her true colors as I expounded on the virtues of obedience training. I knew it was too much to ask for. I did my best to talk out of my mouth even though the speech was slightly going askew, and I was begging Princess to sit in a semi-commanding whisper under my breath. This would have been quite a feat to pull off, even for a person without a speech impediment, but I ended up favoring "Sybil" with an unusual case of Tourette Syndrome. By this time, things were on the verge of spinning out of control and within the blink of an eye, they did. Princess catapulted onto the table by the podium and was diligently using her tongue to wash all the dishes that Sam had used. I gave Sam a helpless look and told Meg to come and control her beast. Unfortunately, they both were laughing so hard, it took them forever to get up and come to my rescue. By then, the whole room was a sea of laughter. Sam, being the gentleman that he was, gingerly put Princess and the scraps on the floor in hopes of helping me regain my train of thought. But it was too late. My speech had long since left the station with no hopes of returning. The only way I could think of to appropriately end this living nightmare was to say, "and this is why you should start obedience classes as early as possible!"

The following year, Meg and I reluctantly went our separate ways. My family had migrated from California back to my grandparents' ranch in Texas, and Meg wanted to move closer to her grandchildren up North. As mentioned before, Meg had outstayed many of the other assistants. According to the U.S. Department of Labor, within the personal assistant field, "turnover is high, a reflection of the relatively low skill requirements, low pay, and high emotional demands of the work." The directcareclearinghouse.org website put out a Literature Review called "The Personal Assistance Services and Direct-Support Workforce" that concurs. Turnover rates are high for direct-care workers in long-term care. The national average of turnover is estimated to be between forty and seventy percent, depending on the facility or service. Most workers leave their jobs within the first year. There are many reasons why people quit after a short time, while others choose to stay longer. But what makes the frequent dismissals or resignations of a personal assistant different from other fields is security. Due to the nature of the job of taking care of someone's personal needs, the relationship between employer and employee is much more intimate. When I say intimate, by no means am I talking sexually. Let's face it, sometimes it may happen, but a normal 9-to-5 job usually does not require an employee to give their boss a shower. That is pretty up close and personal, any way you look at it. Even the issue of showing up to work on time takes on another dimension in the personal assistant service arena. It is not only the principle of punching in on time in order to give the employer a full eight-hour workday. Coming to work on time some days can mean the difference for me in making it to the bathroom in time or having an embarrassing accident. Sometimes an attendant just showing up can mean the difference between eating or not eating that day. So, you can imagine why serious contemplation goes into replacing an assistant. Some may strongly disagree, but sometimes it's easier or more comfortable to stick with a mediocre assistant rather than face the fear of starting all over with the unknown.

One of my major flaws is my hatred of drastic changes. It has been said that I probably would've been one of the last passengers to get off the Titanic because I would have hated to change boats in midstream. Granted, my situation could improve with a new assistant, but there was also a good chance it wouldn't. History has proven that time and time again. Because of this, I prefer to stick to who I know, rather than take the risk of destroying something that is already good.

A year ago, I attended a funeral for a dear friend. I did not expect to take away what I consider to be a pearl of wisdom from such a sad setting, but the preacher spoke on the abundant life, so naturally it caught my attention. He spoke from John 10:10 and said that one definition of abundance "is having too much not to give it away." Of course, he was talking about my friend's jovial personality. She could spread smiles for miles and always seemed to have too much zeal for life not to share it. It was contagious when you were around her. But I got to thinking. Couldn't this go in the opposite direction? For instance, there are times when life feels like nothing but stress and strife. Then, there are times when no matter how well you planned out your life, detours like loss, death, anxiety, or constant change knock you off course. You wake up and go to bed telling God that something's got to give, but you don't have a clue how or what. It's so easy to look for someone else to blame in times when life seems to be swiftly funneling down the drain. All too often we blame those closest to us. Two or more lives can become so enmeshed that they lose the ability to draw clear lines between helping and hindering. In such frustrating times we tend to jump on the things we can change with as little effort as possible.

Although we thoroughly enjoyed four fun-filled years together, the relationship between Meg and I had hit a plateau. She could no longer make me happy and I could not make her happy. When a person works where they live, it is hard to keep personal and work life from becoming entangled. We also made the blunder of having too many unrealistic expectations and depended on each other too much to supply true happiness that could only come from ourselves. Meg and I made the tragic mistake of losing sight that this was indeed a job for her. It's easy to do when one works 24/7 or even 24/5 with the same person for a long period of time. This was sort of the way it was when I let Meg go. I'm not saying it was wrong or right, but all I could see was that getting rid of her was the fastest way to change my life.

And it did. Meg moved back home to be close to her family and watch her grandchildren grow up. Most of them had been born while she was working with me, so she wanted to make up for lost time. I went back home and drove my family crazy until the next victim, or partner-in-crime, came along. Once again, another segment of my life began with the infamous ad. In hopes of speeding up the *process* of waiting for someone with *the right stuff* to apply, mom even placed the ad in papers such as the Baptist Standard. I think my parents secretly hoped we would get an applicant from the Baptist Standard who could tame my wild spirit. We received some very interesting prospects. Some even came from prison inmates promising they could fulfill the job description if I would wait on them to serve out their term. Even though this sounded exciting to me, my parents were not exactly enthusiastic about hiring an ex-convict to take care of their daughter. Parents are funny that way. By now you would think it would be second nature for me to expect the unexpected, but for some reason I kept trying to color people within my lines of comfort. But thank goodness the One who is in control continued to force me to expand those lines and showed me how wonderfully diverse people can be when typecasting does not enter the picture. Each personal assistant added a special depth to my life that I would not have reached otherwise. Some added deep shades of darkness to my life's painting, while others added splashes of radiant brightness that illuminated new areas to explore. Each person moved lines that I thought were firmly drawn in concrete. This shifting perspective has allowed me to gain a stronger sense of self.

I had always heard that preacher's kids were either prudes or wild as March hares, so I was a bit leery when we found out that Amanda was a Southern Baptist preacher's daughter. Fortunately, she did not fit in either category, but I wasn't certain how it was going to work out because she was the first assistant I'd ever had who was younger than me. One thing was for sure. Her energy level was positively younger than mine, and her understanding reached far beyond her age. As you will soon find out, Amanda was definitely a fireball in more ways than one.

Our initial meeting threw me off guard. By this time, I

had moved back to the ranch with my family, so we asked Amanda to fly across the state for an interview and spend a weekend with us. I felt I had to do something impressive to hook her and entice her to stay. But as you've figured out by now, no matter how hard I tried to pull off some of my most impressive "moves," they often turned out like skits from the *Carol Burnett Show*.

In order to appease my hankering to drive, my parents bought a golf cart for me to putter around the ranch in. They knew they had done the right thing by getting me a cart instead of a car the first moment I stepped on the gas pedal. Since all good big sisters take their little sisters for car rides, I thought it would be very appropriate to take mine with me on my first drive. My new, shiny, white cart with the dark, tinted windshield came complete with two rear bucket seats just big enough for two little behinds. My two little sisters climbed on up and got settled in while dad gave me final instructions for lift off. And I do mean lift off! In all of dad's wise instructions, he forgot to mention the fact that it was not necessary to "put the pedal to the metal" upon take off. In fact, accelerating during takeoff can be quite dangerous. At least it proved to be so for my sisters. To quote an onlooker that day, "Golly, you scattered kids for miles and miles." They were so small and light, they were airborne in no time flat. Even their stylish "Captain & Tennille" shag haircuts could not provide a parachute big enough to give a soft landing, but thankfully no one was hurt.

Luckily, by the time Amanda came along I had learned how *not* to catapult my passengers, so I thought I would impress her with my driving skill while dazzling her with conversation. From my perspective, things were rolling along just fine. Amanda was talking and laughing at all of the appropriate times, so I knew she was at least getting most of what I was saying. My confidence level was building each time she agreed with me or we found a common interest. Then I asked her if she wanted to see the horses. I thought it would at least be entertaining for a while and ease the pressure of getting to know each other in a weekend.

We were discussing the way so many beautiful horses have unbelievably hokey names. I was so engrossed in our conversation that it slipped my mind that we were in a golf cart and not a four-wheel drive. Riding across rough desert terrain, or "bajaing" in this part of the country, is not an option in a golf cart. My dad claimed that if he could line up all the holes he has ever dug me out of, he would have a straight shot to China. This was before cell phones, so if and when my cart got stuck, I could be stuck anywhere from five minutes to two hours. Someone would usually pass by in that time and that someone was usually dad. Even though I was always grateful he came to my rescue, I dreaded hearing his "how many times have I told you" speech. This time was certainly no exception, but a bit more embarrassing.

Amanda and I had finished making the rounds to every horse stall and were about to make a U-turn and go back to the house for some iced tea. It was mid-June and the 90-degree heat was steaming up from the black top and sand. We were both unpleasantly beaded with sweat, and everyone knows good southern belles avoid sweating if possible. The harder I pushed on the gas pedal, the hotter it became. While cranking the non-powered steering wheel to make a 180 degree turn up a small incline that led to the hardtop road from the horse stalls, we suddenly felt that sickening, sinking feeling as the back wheels spun deeper and deeper into the soft amber sand. There was absolutely nothing I could do but smile and say "whoops" as charmingly as possible as I gracefully tried to straighten my front tires and reverse. This was so far from the first impression I wanted to make on Amanda that all I could do was laugh. I couldn't help but think every time the back tires sunk deeper and deeper into the sand, "This will really make her want to stay!" Amanda offered to get out and push. What else could I say but, okay. She got out, went around to the back, and said, "On the count of three, gas it."

As she energetically hopped around to the back bumper, I watched her flex her biceps in the side mirrors. Though Amanda would argue about her size, in my eyes she's always been sort of a S.C.U.D missile—small but mighty with an explosively funny personality. I'll never forget the determined look in her huge, dark brown eyes that said, "Okay, we can do this. I am woman, hear me roar!" However, it was amazing how quickly that determined look changed into one of utter disbelief as the sand and dirt clods went flying up her legs, arms, into her mouth and hair, and the rest of her body. Fighting back the urge to explode with nervous laughter, I dared not to look Amanda in the eyes as I suggested she walk back to the house and get my dad to help rescue us. I wish I could claim this was the one and only time we were bogged down in the sand, but as dad often reminds me, "gee, you must really enjoy your mistakes because once is never enough!" Ever since that day, I have heard nothing but disparaging comments about my driving, such as "well, at least you know for sure I did not stick around because of your outstanding driving skills." These sarcastic remarks only escalated after the time Amanda asked me to "hold the wheel and keep it between the lines" while she climbed to the back of the van to get a snack bag. We were on I-40 going towards Oklahoma and as usual, there were a lot of trucks on the road going in our same direction. Don't ask me why, but she got a bit hysterical when she looked up and saw that we were about a long arm's reach from an eighteen-wheeler. I thought we were rolling along just fine because it appeared to me that we were between the lines until she let out a blood-curdling scream. It startled me so much that we came within inches from the massive truck. I never thought a two-foot sprint and a three-foot hurdle could be done so compactly in a Dodge Caravan, but she did both quite impressively. Amanda's athletic ability especially shone that day as she cleared the arm rest and grasped the steering wheel in one fell swoop. Much to Amanda's disbelief, we were fine. We're both still alive to tell the story and that's what counts, isn't it?

Even though Amanda was only with me approximately eighteen months, it took fourteen years for her to vindicate me from her constant reminder that my driving was a threat to society. But it finally came through a delightful pint size replica of her. Her nine-year old son, Brett. They came to visit us for our yearly, sizzling, summer get-together in July of 2003 and graced my home for a few days before we embarked on a long jaunt south to visit their abode. Since Brett had just finished studying about the historic Monahans sandhills that year in school, nothing would satisfy him until we went to visit, which wasn't a big deal because it's close to my place.

It happened to be another ninety plus summer day and there was no shortage of sweat. Believe me, Amanda and I would never have stepped out of the air-conditioned car if we hadn't promised Brett he could go surfing on a large, round, sand disc, down the great dunes of Monahans. As all boys that age do, Brett would not be satisfied until he had conquered the tallest dune. So we were driving around the park trying to find that perfect dune when we came upon about a six-foot sandy place between the blacktop and where we wanted to go. There was a picnic table near-by so we assumed the ground would at least be semi-solid. In Amanda's defense, the sand looked like it was packed down hard enough to drive on. But like many mirages, it was a nasty trick of the desert! We got about half-way across to the black top road and that old familiar sinking feeling came over us. When Amanda realized we were not on solid rock but on sinking sand, she quickly tried to back up. But it was like the hymn says, there was "no turning back, no turning back!" Poor little Brett stepped out of the side door and told us not to worry, he would dig us out while we called the friendly Park Ranger. At that moment, I had déjà vu of the time his mother tried to push a golf cart out of the sand with all of her small might. Though I must say, Brett did it with a bit more finesse. He got down on all fours and dug like a mad dog behind the back tires. When he saw that it was futile, he sat on the edge of the deep, sandy ridge where the tires had spun out and exclaimed, "we're stuck!" It was another one of those Lucy & Ethel situations where our predicament was so unbelievable that all we could do was laugh. Of course, just as I predicted, Amanda tried to tell the ranger that I was driving when we got stuck. Since he was obviously a person with a good sense of humor, he told Amanda that she should have never let me take the wheel. I could not resist. I said. "yes, you know how we people are: Give us a mile and we'll get stuck in it every time!" Despite his sharp tongue and wit, we were glad he was able to tow us out with one smooth jolt.

By this hour of the day, we had decided we would pay whatever it took unless it was astronomically expensive because we had already used our "get out of jail free" pass that morning with my dad. Earlier, I had forgotten the battery charger to my chair. I learned the hard way to never leave home without it unless I have the sadistic desire to truly be stuck. Like a modern-day hero, dad in his white sports car and his trusty companion, Samona, a Great Pyrenees, was kind enough to bring it to us at the halfway marker. We realized the grave mistake of forgetting the only power source for my chair when we arrived halfway between the house and Monahans. Though my house was only thirty minutes behind us, we still had about a nine hour drive to Amanda's house. So, the idea of turning around and re-tracing thirty minutes was very unappealing, not to mention tragic for one nine-year old boy who had waited three days to surf the sand dunes.

There was absolutely no good time to be stuck in my shiny, new, forest green van, especially on that day. We always seem to be inconvenienced when we're in a rush to get from one point to the next. But in life, it's not just dirt holes we get stuck in. Sometimes it's bad habits, sins, traffic jams, pity parties, etc. Our gut reaction is to roll our eyes heavenward in exasperation. Could it be that God uses those exasperating experiences to focus our eyes on him, if only for a moment? Getting stuck can be a part of the abundant life that is not at all pleasant, but it may be the best way that God has to get our attention. Once he has it, he can work all things out for good. I fully realize that getting my new van stuck at the Monahans Sandhills State Park is in no way an earth-shattering crisis. But it did happen on a day when we still had nine hours to go in ninety plus degree weather. It was inconvenient to say the least, but we did make some priceless memories that day.

It's obvious by now that we hired Amanda to be my personal assistant, but let's pick back up where we left off, shall we? The weekend she came to visit was full of sunbeams, dirt clods and information. By the time dad and I took her back to the airport to catch a flight home, we were both ready to get back to our corners of Texas and think on whether this would be a good fit. Don't get me wrong. I was ready to sign a contract before she boarded the plane, but I don't think she was ready. At least, that was the impression I got when we arrived at the terminal and she quickly thanked us for a nice weekend, turned around, and walked off with absolutely no indication of a yes or no about taking the job. It was one of the strangest goodbyes I had ever taken part in. I don't know what I expected her to say, but silence was not it. I was hoping for an answer or a clear sign of which direction she was leaning. Other than getting stuck in ninety-degree weather at the stinky horse pens, I thought the weekend had gone smoothly. There were those few awkward moments of silence but nothing out of the ordinary for a lengthy first-time meeting. I so much wanted an indication of Amanda's intentions I thought that I must have surely missed something.

I made dad push my manual chair over to where she was waiting to board the plane and said, "I just wanted to thank you again for coming and for the great time. I hope that we have a chance to have many more!" To my dismay and frustration, Amanda smoothly said something to the effect of, "Thanks. Really enjoyed it, too." I wheeled away still wondering where she stood on the possibility of coming back. It wasn't until sixteen years later that I came to realize and appreciate what she was doing. She rarely does much without weighing all the consequences. She is spunky and spontaneous, but never rash. We all reach a time in our lives when we get tired of making mistakes and want a "clean break" from old habits so that we can to prove to ourselves that we can indeed start over from the ashes. God says that He will turn our ashes into beauty, but it's hard to believe when we are in the midst of the flames. (Isaiah 61:3) Amanda's heart was tender and bruised from some choices she'd made in the past. She wanted a new start, a complete change of scenery, but she wanted to be sure this was the right place to start fresh. Being my personal assistant was a big responsibility with some major sacrifices for a twenty-six year-old. She looked at me with her compassionate, dark eyes as she tried to fully size up the impending situation. Knowing Amanda as well as I do now, I believe facts were flowing fast and furiously through her head. I can just imagine her asking, "Lord, am I truly up for this? After all I've been through, do you really want me to get "stuck" with her?" I cannot speak for Amanda, but our friendship has been a priceless gift from God.

Chapter 4
1988-1990

And they say I'm the one with the disability?

I have been fortunate so far with the connections I've had with my assistants. Because of the lack of stability in the field of personal assistant care, when I find someone who is truly enjoyable to live with, it's hard to let them go. The relationships that evolve into lasting friendships have proven to be few and far between. If you consider that I'm now in my early forties and the first assistant came to me when I was four, this gives you some idea of the revolving door of people in and out of my life. Some assistants last less than four hours, while one lasted almost five years. It never fails; the ones I become closest to always go too soon. Flavia, a well-known contemporary inspirational artist and writer, sums it up best: "some come and go quickly through our lives, others stay for a while and leave footprints on our hearts and we are never ever the same."

Whether we're talking about footprints on my heart or wheel prints in the sand, Amanda has definitely made a lasting impression! Though she was only with me for a short time before she was rescued by her knight in shining armor, we crammed many nutty escapades in the time we had together. The perplexed feeling I had over our first farewell at the airport was just an inkling of the ways Amanda caused me to color outside of the comfortable boundaries I had drawn for myself. Because she was the first assistant who was younger than me, I was expected to play a more mature role than in the past. There were some responsibilities I gladly embraced, and others I didn't. I was more than happy to be a warm place to rely on when the world was cold for Amanda. However, when it came to self-sufficiency and happiness for myself, she really pushed me to color outside my lines. We had quite a few heated discussions about depending on someone else to be the total source for one's emotional and physical needs. She was mature for her age and was accustomed to relying on God and herself to meet her needs. To put it mildly, I was not. Having older personal assistants for the majority of my life made it very easy for me to fall into the irresponsible child role. It would be simple to claim that I was just too lazy and spoiled to do more for myself in vital life skill areas but being emotionally and physically dependent on others was actually an escape from the reality of having a disability. When I depended on others to fulfill my crucial needs, I could blame others if I had a bad day or was late for class. That was my assistant's job. It was easy to evade responsibility because I wasn't bound by my limitations, but by my assistant's. On the other hand, when it came to strength, I felt bulletproof because not only did I have mine, but I capitalized on theirs as well. This mentality did not fly with Amanda. She not only wanted me to be accountable for my own emotional needs and accept responsibility for the physical ones I could handle, but also willingly provide for some of hers, too. In other words, she wanted a give-and-take relationship.

Amanda took time to have a life for herself when it was possible. Though this was perfectly natural and logical, it was almost impossible for me not to be envious. Her gregarious nature made her a people magnet, the life of the party. Everybody wanted to take her out or just be around her. So, in an odd way, I was both jealous of her ability to attract all types of people, and envious of her affections towards them. On top of this, she wanted me to willingly give her the time off that she was due and have a gracious attitude about it. Not that it was an unreasonable request, but the concept was indeed coloring outside of my lines! Despite the fact that it has taken many years and tears to distinguish boundaries between asking for what the job requires, versus the unrealistic expectation that my personal assistant would want me around most of her waking hours, Amanda has stood by me as I've fought to keep that line intact. Not that I really wanted to be around someone twenty-four hours a day, but being with them helped me ignore the realization of my limitations. I could keep up a false sense of self. But this façade was eventually stripped all the way down.

I will never forget how honored and mature I felt when mom and dad asked me to house sit while they went out of town. As I mentioned before, Amanda and I had a knack for turning the mundane and ordinary into the opposite. Every day was like an episode from a Lucy & Ethel, or Laverne & Shirley show. When my parents asked us to house sit, we hadn't planned to have wild parties or to use their house to conduct "risky business." But their household was definitely at risk when they left the two of us in charge.

I had invited one of my oldest and dearest girlfriends, Lynn, over for a slumber party, but at the wise old age of twenty-eight, our idea of partying was catching up on all the local gossip, watching horror flicks in our comfy pajamas, and stuffing our faces until we lost consciousness, either from laughing or passing out from a self-induced food coma. Lynn's tall, dark, and handsome husband Jed was working the night shift that week at the local gas plant, so she was free to go out after he left for work. Believe it or not, gentle Jed was glad that Lynn was spending the night with us because he hated to leave her alone at night. Though Lynn was mighty in mouth and kept all of us in uproarious laughter, she was only five foot two, with opaque baby blue eyes, and often startled by her own shadow.

Eating is a very important part of mine and Amanda's world. Her husband Bailey claims that we are the Dessert

Demolition Queens because we order three or four desserts to one entrée. We've tried over and over to explain the well-known fact that when God created dessert on the seventh day, he not only said that it was very good, but that desserts were meant to be thoroughly savored and shared. Upon arrival at my parents' place, we had a few hours before Lynn showed up for the movie madness marathon, so we began collecting a smorgasbord of delectable snacks. Finding the good stuff was easy in my folks' kitchen because mom always had a well-stocked pantry for just-in-case scenarios. In the rush of it all, Manda and I decided to create a frozen orange juice concoction that was supposed to be melt-in-your-mouth-goodness. To accompany this frightfully festive evening, we turned on some classic tunes, such as *Heard It Through the Grapevine*, to heighten and inspire our culinary skills. Amanda was rhythmically tossing ingredients into the blender with a wooden spoon, while I was grooving and singing. By the time my parents got home, we were still picking tiny wooden splinters out of the ceiling and cleaning up telltale traces of orange juice off the cabinet doors. So this is why you don't use a wooden spoon in a blender! We made it through the rest of "fright night" disaster free, but it was hard to tell which was scarier—the movies or the amount of food we devoured.

Over the next few days, Amanda and I laughed and wondered whether consuming eight hours of classic horror movies jinxed the rest of our stay. We had already cleaned up orange juice and wooden shavings off the kitchen cabinets and ceilings, so we thought the worst part of mopping up messes was over. Boy, were we wrong! Knowing the dangerous minds of my two cohorts, I expected one of them to jump out from behind the shower curtain wildly waving a butter knife while I was indisposed in the bathroom! *Psycho* had always been an inspirational movie for them. If they had stooped to such shenanigans, it would have given new meaning to "being caught with my pants down." Not putting anything past those two, I kept one eye in the mirror and the other one to watch where I was driving my wheelchair. I slowly crept up to the sink to wash my hands. As usual, my hands unsteadily groped for the ornate swan faucet that mom had special ordered when my parents did some remodeling on my grandparents' house. It was indeed beautiful but not conducive for everyday use. The long, graceful, curved neck flowed to an open beak which served as the actual faucet, with etched wing handles that controlled the water temperature. After I finished, Amanda came in to give me a helping hand. In the process of washing my hands, I reached for a wing. I was sure I didn't pull hard enough on the wing to break it off, but somehow the handle would not let go of my hand. As sure as I live, I've never seen water change directions so fast and furiously. The water went from calm to gushing in a matter of seconds! It was almost as phenomenally forceful as Old Faithful.

Amanda let out a blood curdling-scream and turned into

a human spinning top. She made a mad dash for the towel cabinet and quickly grabbed towels to cover the new bathroom fountain while glaring at me as if I was the guilty party and had a murder weapon in my hand. Then, she looked at me as if I were Lassie the dog and was supposed to go and find help. I was baffled because Lynn had left right before this little incident, so the dogs and horses were the only species around. I did the only logical thing that I could think of. I called Jackson, my second father, who was thirty miles away. If fools rush in where angels fear to tread, I must be a big fool. I cannot even begin to remember all of the goofy jokes I mischievously played on this man. But one thing is for sure, Jackson and his wife Josie loved me as one of their own. He worked for my dad for thirty-five years before retiring and going into the ministry. I guess that is why I had the nerve to call him on a peaceful Saturday afternoon to come and be a hero and rescue us from the disaster we created.

I didn't have any siblings until I was nine, so their three kids became my brother and sisters. I've always stuck out in a crowd, but I really stuck out when I was with them, and it wasn't just because of my severe disability. I am on the opposite end of the color spectrum. They are rich, delicious, dark chocolate and I am scrumptious white, but we are both undeniably classic Godiva chocolates! Since my dad's idea of roughing it was bad service at the MGM hotel in Vegas, my parents were never big on camping out. Jackson and Josie had mercy on me and let me invade several of their camping trips.

In fact, it was because of them that I was a full-fledged Girl Scout and had earned several camping badges. So what if I bent the rules and slept in a heated Winnebago. I still got the badge. But as I grew older, my appreciation for the great outdoors vastly increased. So, as a surprise several years later, Jackson bought a very nice, green, deluxe tent to set up by the river so he and I could fall asleep listening to the rushing water. He figured at least one of his adventurous grandchildren would enjoy having a space of their own to camp in.

Six summers before the gushing water catastrophe, I went camping with the family. As usual, Jackson was up at the crack of dawn making coffee over an open fire. Since I don't believe that God intended movement to occur before 9:00 a.m., Jackson was kind enough to let me sleep in a bit. Arising from my coma, I heard a group of men around the campfire, laughing and chewing the fat over a steaming cup of joe. Jackson was a people magnet and never met a stranger. Once he met someone, they were friends for life. I lay quietly in my sleeping bag for a few minutes taking in the wonderful smells of the woods, the fresh brewed coffee, and the sounds of jovial conversation. Not wanting to interrupt a good thing, I debated whether to make my awakened presence known, or just lie there a bit longer and wait for a lull in their banter. I didn't have to think about it for very long. Suddenly, an eyeball peered into a crack of the fabric tent door. Jackson vigorously unzipped the tent door.

"Good morning, Sunshine," he said in a booming voice,

as he tenderly lifted me from the sleeping bag. The tent was fairly large and sturdy but getting me up and out of such a confining space was no small feat. It wobbled to and fro as we jerkily two stepped to the door. I could see four or five guys still standing around the campfire through the bellowing flap over the unzipped tent door. They appeared to be middle aged to older men who were engrossed in their coffee talk until we came out of the tent. You could have heard a leaf crackle when we burst forth from our unzipped green cocoon. Their expressions read like they were the deer and we were the headlights. Not only was I the "wrong" color but I was a young female with a disability. I could see their expressions change from shock, to curiosity, then amazement. Meanwhile, as Jackson situated me in my chair in all of my glorious beauty, they suddenly remembered all sorts of chores that they needed to finish at their campers.

I couldn't resist the awkwardness of the moment and said, "Gee, thank you for such a fun night. Hope it was good for you, too." In all of my days I've never seen old geezers scatter so fast!

Poor Jackson turned a shade of embarrassment, shrugged his broad shoulders, and sighed, "Can't take you anywhere."

I've always had an irresistible urge to embarrass this incredibly gentle giant. I remember Jackson devoting an afternoon in early December to take me Christmas shopping. In the early 70s, racism was more pronounced than it is now. It was not as common to see biracial families or "mixed company" as it is today, so naturally, we received a few strange glances as we shopped. By now, you know I couldn't just let it go. The stranger the looks, the bigger the show! Sometimes I would grab Jackson's large, dark hand and hold it as we strolled through the mall. If I felt that they deserved a grand eye-opening treatment, I would grab his jolly, chubby cheeks, kiss him right on the lips and say, "Oh, I love you so much, daddy." It was so much fun to watch people squirm, then power walk away as quickly as possible, trying as hard as they could to resist another quick glance of incredulity. Or was it disgust? Either way, Jackson and his wife, Josie never said a discouraging word to me and always came to my rescue when I called. I could hear trepidation in his voice that day as I tried to explain that I'd de-winged mom and dad's fancy faucet.

"You did what?" Jackson asked.

"I didn't mean to, but the swan's wing came off in my hand and now water is shooting up from its armpit and now the whole room is flooding! Can you please come over now?"

Of course, he had no clue what I was talking about, or that swans had armpits, so he requested to speak to Amanda. After gathering the facts, he explained to her how to turn off the main water valve from under the sink. By the time Amanda had successfully shut the water off, my mom's beautiful bathroom looked as if a small river had run through it!

After we soaked up the massive puddles of water on the floor, and Jackson "healed" the wing by laying hands on it, we felt we were surely on the home stretch. My folks would be back in twenty-four hours and all we had to do was ride the wave of time and not turn anything else on. Jackson told us to call if we needed anything else, but Amanda and I were certain he was hoping we would just sit tight and not make any more messes. In theory it sounded good, but considering our track record, it was highly unlikely. Later on that same afternoon, the clock and the animals told us that it was feeding time. As we were filling up the food pans outside, I noticed that it *felt* strange, even though everything looked as if it was in order. I brushed it off and blamed it on the all-night horror movie marathon, which always messes with my head the day afterwards. We headed inside and went straight to the den and gazed out of the wall of windows that overlooked parts of the front and back yards. While scanning the yards to make sure we had done everything on our checklist, my dad's office door caught my eye. It seemed odd to me that the door would be ajar with dad being gone for four days, but I figured he left it cracked for ventilation. Maybe Jackson or one of the day workers might have left it open by mistake. In any case, I thought Amanda should check it out to ensure my safety. One never knows who or what might be lurking in the shadows! She swears that I set it all up just to scare the bejeezus out of her, but I promise on my soul that I did no such thing. However, it would have been a great practical joke!

At that time, my parent's motley crew of dogs consisted of a Lab, a Chow, two Basset Hounds, a Mutt, and Princess, my trusty Rottweiler. Like every good guard dog that has remarkable instincts for showing up at feeding time but disappearing in perilous times, these dogs were true professionals. I assured Amanda that Princess or Brook, mom's black Lab, would be more than happy to accompany her in the face of danger. We agreed that it would be best if I stayed where I was with the phone in my lap so I could call the police if she did not come back, or at least stick her head out of the office door within five minutes. Keep in mind, this was about twelve years pre-emergency phone number, 911, so if indeed we had a crisis on our hands, things would certainly have quickly gone to the dogs because my folks had neither a redial button nor speed dial on their phone. After one last rehearsal of our operating procedures for the worst-case scenario, Amanda drew a deep breath and hesitantly opened the den door.

Before stepping off the den porch into the great unknown, she slowly eyeballed the yard then closed the door behind her. She went down the top step on her left foot then cleared the next two with a swift hop. For the sake of any onlookers, Amanda was trying to display an air of carefree confidence but I knew that she was shaking in her sneakers. From my bird's eye view, I could see she was making her way towards dad's office. A light bulb appeared to suddenly go on inside of her head. Her ebony eyes almost bulged out of her head as she seemed to realize that she was approaching a possible foe without a weapon. She made a sudden U-turn, flew up the steps, and bounded into the house exclaiming that she could not believe that she went out there weaponless. I fought back the urge to ask if the terrifying look on her face wouldn't do the trick of scaring the predator and sending them running to the next county, but I valued breathing so I really did not want to be the one on whom the weapon was dispatched.

Without much thought, I showed Amanda where dad kept the key to the gun cabinet. She was now armed and very dangerous because the first thing she grabbed was dad's long rifle. One look at her would probably send our prowler running for his or her life since he or she was in grave danger of laughing themselves to death. Watching her hold the extra-long barrel rifle instantly made me think of Barney Fife and Elmer Fudd. With a bit more bravery and determination in her step, Amanda once again swung open the den door and bounded down the steps. In spite of her newfound confidence, she still called all the dogs to escort her into the office. Naturally, both Amanda and I expected the two bigger dogs, Princess and Brook, to lead the procession into the dimly lit office, but once again they announced their indispensable bravery by allowing the smaller dogs to make their grand entrance first. It gave us an eerie feeling when Brook and Princess quickly backed away from the door as Amanda reached for the doorknob, but I shrugged it off and blamed it on their idol worship of Scooby-Doo. But when my dad's ferocious mutt backed away with her tail tucked as the door opened, we all paused. Watching Amanda march into the office like a dead woman walking was nerve-wracking enough, but when she and the Bassett hounds didn't come out of the door after five minutes, I became as nervous as Garfield when faced with an empty refrigerator. My total concentration was on that office door. Five minutes felt like fifteen minutes and counting. Little did I know that the anxiety I felt was nothing compared to the panic Amanda was feeling when she looked behind door number two. As I said previously, the brave but very short Bassets, Cleopatra and DeeDee, were the only ones who barged in as if they were large and in charge. Their long, brown, velvety ears were bouncing off the ground while their noses were working overtime, sniffing as they trotted towards the second room in the office.

Everything seemed copasetic in the front of the office until DeeDee stopped at the end of a steel-toed rain boot, sat down and looked straight up. The boot was sticking out from the bottom of the door to the supply room. Chills ran up Amanda's spine as she followed DeeDee's lead. She really didn't want to look and behold what was behind the door, but she also didn't want to be ambushed. Her eyes, wide as saucers, slowly traveled upwards until they landed on a yellow slicker. By this time all she wanted to do was run. She had no desire to meet a yellow slicker killer, but she made her eyes do the walking on up the buttonholes to the collar. She took a quick glance and saw that a cowboy hat adorned the hood connected to the collar. The dark brim hung low and shadowed the face so much that it favored an uninviting black hole. Amanda shuddered to think of what she would see next and stepped back into the other room to gather her wits, all the while thinking she should run like crazy. Common sense seemed to have fled the scene because if there was indeed a Freddie Kruger on the loose, wearing a yellow slicker and a cowboy hat, she should have been gone a long time ago.

Amanda grasped the edge of the desk as if to gather her courage before thrusting herself back into the lion's den to meet her foe. With one deep breath that seemed to propel her across the room and into the dreaded doorway, she rushed back to DeeDee's side. Realizing that the rifle was still tightly clutched in her hand, she mustered up the guts to say, "Hello, anyone there?" I agree that it was a stupid thing to say but doesn't this come out of someone's mouth in almost every horror movie? Anyway, after receiving the silent treatment, Amanda trudged onward. Neither the rain boots or the slicker had budged an inch since the last viewing, so she concluded that it was time to take one last big step and look into the face of danger.

"You may be silent, but I've been known to be deadly," she cried out as she stomped into the room. To solidify her claim, she raised the rifle at the strange figure and accidentally hit the very tip of the cowboy hat that was hiding most of the face. As she made the hundred-yard dash out the office, I heard her screaming wildly, "Oh my gosh! I've knocked his head clean off with this gun." Not expecting to hear this, it took me a minute to comprehend the gravity of the situation. As she gave me a step by step replay, we both came to the same conclusion at approximately the same time. You see, what appeared to be a black hole under the cowboy hat was indeed just that. One of the workers obviously went a bit overboard and thought he would melt without protection. So, he had neatly hung his rain gear on a tall hat rack that stood just inside the second office door. He completed the ensemble with his hat and rain boots. The main thing I fought that day was the urge to laugh uncontrollably, but I thought laughter at that moment might not have been wisest thing to do, especially given the fact that Amanda was still clutching dad's double barrel shotgun. It would have been one thing if we had only jeopardized the sink. Water eventually dries. But it was quite another when Amanda played with fire in our own home.

* * *

Christmas was mine and Amanda's favorite holiday. I love all the festivities around that time of year. Since we had just moved into a new townhouse the previous summer, we were quite eager to decorate and entertain guests for the holidays. Amanda started a list in November for everyone we needed to shop for, then we made another list of the things we wanted to accomplish before

Christmas. Believe me, it's a good thing that we started the early part of November. While I'd be busy cramming for finals, Amanda would be in the kitchen creating new concoctions that she'd dreamt of in class, instead of taking notes for me. Thank goodness I paid attention during class because note taking was not her specialty. She was quite spectacular at doodling names and menus, though.

Sometimes when she was really bored, Amanda would cleverly hold up a notebook or a newspaper in front of her face as though she were truly interested in what she was reading, but I was not fooled. I knew that Amanda was catching a few Z's. I was jealous because she could discreetly nod off at the drop of a hat (if she did not snore). I sat on the front row so I could never get away with it, especially if I started my Olympic drooling. My Boxers are the only ones who truly have an appreciation for that skill!

Amanda loved to make all sorts of Christmas goodies from new recipes that she'd discovered in magazines. The more complex a recipe was, the more she liked it because it challenged her culinary skills. I never complained. There was no doubt about it. I would rather eat Amanda's good cooking any day than read over boring class notes. So that day as I studied in my room, I heard Amanda yell. I figured she was just checking to see if I was still alert behind closed doors because I was notorious for falling asleep with my face literally in a book in the afternoons. Amanda's fiancé Bailey was over for a visit one day and caught me coming out of my room.

He unfortunately felt the need to converse and asked what the dark stuff on my forehead was. After close investigation, Amanda almost died laughing when she made out some words from a textbook that had been imprinted on my face while I was sleeping. Though I repeatedly tried telling them that learning by osmosis was the latest technique and the knowledge was going straight to my brain through the skin on my forehead, they did not buy it. Regretfully, they are the kind of friends who will take great pleasure in reminding me of this incident until the day I die.

Amanda had been grilling, baking, and everything else on that December day. We were having guests over that evening and as usual, Amanda had cooked enough to feed "the five thousand." She yelled again, but this time she sounded serious. I heard footsteps walking quickly towards my room. Before I could get my wheelchair turned around, the door flew open and there stood Amanda. Her entrance reminded me of Kramer on *Seinfield*.

She greeted me hysterically asking, "Look at my eyes. Are my eyes all right!?"

"Yes, yea, why? What happened?"

"And my hair. Is my hair okay?"

"Yes," I said. "What did you do? Oh my, your eyebrows. What did you do?!"

"For real!? Are my eyebrows gone? I was tired of waiting for the grill to get hot, so I dashed more lighter fluid on the smoldering coals and WHOOSH, it lit right up! In fact, two great balls of fire shot up and almost caught the house on fire. Guess the flames singed my eyebrows."

I did my best not to laugh, but Amanda's high forehead and big, dark eyes without eyebrows made her look like an alien. After a brief investigation to discover that she and our abode were still intact, all I could think of was "goodness, gracious, great balls of fire!"

Not too long after that grilling experience, another near mishap occurred. Home insurance might not have been a bad idea in those days. This time it was my eyebrows that were almost singed. Finals were over and I finally rolled out of my hole without any dark impressions on my forehead. We invited one of our best friends over to celebrate with dinner and gifts before we left to be with our own families for the holidays. As usual, our home was decked out to the nth degree. Amanda had decorated it in great detail. Nothing escaped her decorative touch—from the tree to the napkin rings on the table. She had even filled an old wicker platter that was a high school graduation gift with red candles and ferns. It looked beautifully festive with all of the fresh cut greenery arranged around the sparkling candles sitting on a square heavy table in our small entryway. I was in my room primping when our friend Mel drove up. Mel was my cute, blue-eyed, petite, mild mannered friend with a loving personality. It felt as if Santa himself with a sleigh full of goodies had blown in. Amanda yelled and told me that she was going to play elf and help Mel carry some packages in from her car. Because she was short with a slight build and no eyebrows, Amanda fit the bill for an elf quite well. She had not been out of the front door ten minutes when I began to smell a funny, smoky odor accompanied by a faint, crackling noise. Immediately thinking that Amanda was trying to singe something else off, I swung open my bedroom door and you guessed it. The greenery around, and on the table was engulfed in flames. If the flames weren't extinguished soon, the platter would go up in a blaze of glory.

Amanda and Mel claim that I spoke in tongues that evening. One might say even my lips became spastic as I tried to scream "FIRE!" But they were too far away to hear me. As they came closer, they thought I was simply waving at them like a wild woman when in actuality, I was trying to relay the urgency of the situation. It was like a bad April Fool's joke except we were months away from April and this wasn't a joke.

When they finally made it inside, Amanda and Mel didn't see the fire because it was angled behind the front door but the flames were getting higher and almost reached the wall that was behind it. Finally, they smelled smoke and figured out it was coming from somewhere else other than our brains. Amanda turned around just in time to see one big poof of fire go straight up the wall. At the sight of the flame and the shocked look on Amanda's face, I couldn't help but say, "And they say *I'm* the one with the disability, Miss Pyromaniac. Goodness gracious, great balls of fire."

Chapter 5
1990-1992

It was wonderful...I think.

've mentioned before that change was hard for me back then, especially when I had a compatible assistant. Just when Amanda and I were making long-term plans to grow old together, her knight in shining armor rode into the picture on a white steed wearing a white baseball cap with an offering of flowers.

Bailey.

He was tall and tanned, with sandy brown hair, and deep green eyes, handsome. He was very polite but the poor guy didn't have a chance with me because I had predetermined that he was a threat to my future happiness. Amanda and Bailey had dated seriously in college but had taken different paths after college. When their paths crossed again, they risked it all. I'm not sure if it was better or worse that they had a quick courtship. All I could think of was how much I dreaded the familiar blast of air coming from the revolving door that was sure to come once they got married. It dawned on me that not only did I feel the danger of losing the security of living with my best friend, but I was also about to graduate with a Bachelor of Arts degree, and desperately needed Amanda's help to make my mark in the real world. My heart kept telling me there was no way that I was meant to move back home after stretching out a four year degree into seven. I had taken my time and had lots of frivolous fun along the way. A loving God wouldn't allow my progression to turn into regression, would He? It never dawned on me that it could all be part of the abundant life they don't talk about either. Leave it to a man to mess up the master plan!

Bailey didn't understand why my stomach dropped at the thought of Manda walking out of our door for the last time. Whisking Amanda away on a white horse meant the old ad would once again be placed on several strategic sites to attract a UFO (Unsuspecting Female Organism). And Lord knows how many would pass through before I found someone who was as compatible with me as Amanda. Furthermore, the gap between her departure and the new-comer's arrival would probably mean a move back to my parents' house in the interval. From a totally selfish point of view, it felt as if Bailey was not only asking for the ultimate sacrifice of giving up my best friend, but also putting my life on hold. Thank goodness he's a sweet-spirited, patient man because I sure gave him a run for his money. He could have been one of the best guys since Jesus Christ walked the earth, and I still would have found some defect in him. Despite my scheming efforts to dislike him, his whimsical nutty charm made him like the brother I never had. However, our bond didn't form overnight. It took a rather large icebreaker to melt me! You could say it happened as subtly as the sinking of the Titanic.

There were guests crawling out of the woodworks from two households when I graduated from the University of Texas at the Permian Basin with my bachelor's degree. That weekend was truly one of the most amazing and joyful times in my life. It reminded me of an episode straight from *This Is Your Life*. People I hadn't seen in many years came from great distances just to see me wheel across the stage. I guess they all wanted to witness a modem day miracle!

When the crowd thinned and the days of celebrating had simmered down, a group from our house decided to go out for yogurt. We figured all of our gluttonous feasting could be erased with one healthy snack. Our table was buzzing with three or four lively conversations at once when suddenly there was an unusual hush at the table. Bailey broke the silence and very politely asked, "Jonean, what is it that you have?"

Not realizing he was serious, I answered, "A headache."

Poor Bailey, trying to be so sincere, said "No, really, what do you call the condition that you have?"

I was slightly taken aback because I'd assumed Amanda had surely filled him in on the gory details of my life by that time. I hesitantly gave a brief neurological description of my specific type of cerebral palsy. I could see the wheels turning in his head as he asked a few more questions and attempted to absorb all of the new information.

The conversation grew a tad too serious for my taste, so I quickly wracked my brain for a topic that would get me out of the hot seat. I looked intently in Bailey's eyes as if I had some more useful information that would perhaps help him come to a better understanding of my disability and asked, "Now Bailey, tell me again, what is it that you have?" And so began our perpetually, petty game of sarcastic paybacks.

Bailey wasted no time getting his bride-to-be back to east Texas and far away from my potentially evil influence. As if I had that much power. They were meant, or doomed, to be together, much like peanut butter and chocolate were made to be combined into irresistible Reese's cups.

In July, Amanda broke the news that she would be leaving on the first of September and I would need to fulfill my duties as her maid of honor in October. I excitedly, but also pathetically, grasped tightly to the honor for fear that it might be the last chance to have a part in Amanda's life.

* * *

The wedding was beautiful and simple. The joy that radiated from them filled the sanctuary with sweet light. Pure, unadulterated relief radiated from every core of my pores when I made it through the ceremony without dropping my bouquet or the ring. With tears of joy and silly, fearful sorrow, I waved goodbye with the crowd of well-wishers as they happily sped away in their candy apple red Firebird Trans Am. I'm glad to say my fears have been allayed by their continual loving friendship and wacky escapades.

In *The Purpose Driven Life,* Rick Warren makes a statement that sounds all too familiar. "Many Christians misinterpret Jesus' promise of the abundant life to mean perfect health, a comfortable lifestyle, constant happiness, full realization of your dreams, and instant relief from problems through faith and prayer. In a word, they expect the Christian life to be easy. They expect heaven on earth." This statement certainly described what I thought Christian life should be at that time. After all, I was already bearing my cross by living with a disability, so why couldn't I have a compatible personal assistant so I could live my life without interruption?

The dreaded day Amanda left, I went back home to my folks' house but kept our place for another month in hopes of finding another assistant to help me before the lease ended. A few times during that month, dad or mom would drop me off at the townhouse I shared with Amanda while they ran errands. I truly don't know if that was the wisest thing to do because I felt totally ambiguous about where I belonged. At the time, I didn't have a van equipped with a ramp or a lift, so I couldn't take my electric chair with me. If I wanted to move from room to room, my hands and knees would have to do the walking. Most of my valuables, such as the computer, television, etc., had already been shuffled back to my folks' house for everyday use so there wasn't much to do at the townhouse.

The majority of our friends had respectable daytime jobs, so the option of hanging out with them while I was in town was slim to none. Though we all had the best intentions of staying in touch, it was tough to do even when I moved only an hour and a half away. Going back to the townhome was a terrible idea. All I truly succeeded in doing was magnifying the good times and minimizing the bad. I was missing Amanda more and more with each look around the house and being sucked deeper into a tornado of self-pity.

One afternoon after mom dropped me off, I was crawling from Manda's old room to the den when I lost what little balance I possess and had a face-to-carpet experience. As I lay on the light beige short shag carpet trying to decide whether it was worth the effort to try and get up or just wait until mom came back to help me, the same treacherous thought that had haunted me throughout my lifetime came for yet another visit. It would be tough for me to estimate how many times a week I'd think or say, "It's not supposed to be this way." In fact, I would be very hard pressed to remember a more self-defeating thought that has plagued my mind and soul. Replaying it in my mind for years created a deep, treacherous groove where it became all too easy to convince myself my life didn't measure up to others. The thought reminded me of the top rim of a tornado building up speed as it travels fast and furiously down the path of self-destruction. The more I focused on negative thoughts, the faster and more destructive my tornado became, threatening to suck my soul right out of my body.

It is at this point when I, and many of you, come face to face with the question of being. It's a frighteningly deadly place to be stuck. If you're anything like me, when we pull out of this dark place and step back to catch our breath, we gain a different perspective and realize it is pretty presumptuous of us to think our life is not supposed to be the way it is since we were never privy to the original blueprints of our masterpiece in the first place. How do we know our life is not exactly what it was intended to be?

The apostle Paul had a gift for putting those of us who had gotten confused or "too big for their britches" back in their places. He wrote, "But indeed, O man, who are you to reply against God? Will the thing formed say to him who formed it, 'Why have you made me like this?'"

Even when God's presence seems to be nowhere on our radar screen of senses and we have no clue of what He is up to, He is always shaping and preparing us for a specific purpose that only we can fulfill. In the book of Job, God lets us have a sneak peek on a domestic dispute between Job and his wife. Job's dear wife thought she knew the answer to helping him out of his misery by suggesting he "curse God and die." For some of us, her advice seems like a viable answer. After all, if we were covered from head to toe in painful oozing sores as Job was, it would stand to reason that we would do anything for relief. But Job gives her a very interesting and insightful answer after he tells her how foolish she is. He replies, "Shall we indeed accept good from God, and not accept adversity?" The scripture states, "in all this Job did not sin from his lips." (Job 2:9,10)

If we believe God is a good and benevolent Lord, it's difficult for us to grasp why He would allow baffling hardships to come our way. But in our purely human state, when do we tend to learn the most? Don't we vividly remember the lessons learned the hard way, more than the ones that came easily to us? The difficult lessons are the ones that leave an indelible mark in our memory and hearts. When life is cruising smoothly along, I tend to take a lot for granted. I don't question or search for meaning in good times as much as I do in rough times. Job realized he had to take the bad along with the good because they come as a packaged deal. We cannot expect one without the other because God uses both good and bad situations to shape us into all that we are meant to be.

Once, when my wise baby sister came home for a visit, we discussed at great length, while fixing my hair, that if one never experienced grief or pain, how would one know and understand joy? Therefore, it makes sense for God to lead us into situations that allow us to experience the opposite emotion to the same degree for a point of reference. I believe this is an aspect of what it means to have an abundant life through Christ.

Another valuable nugget of knowledge we can get from Job is to remember that not every bad thing that happens to us is a direct consequence of our past sins. In Job 2:3, God questions Satan, "Have you considered My servant Job, that there is none like him on the earth, a blameless and upright man, one who fears God and shuns evil? And still he holds fast to his integrity, although you incited Me against him, to destroy him without cause."

In John 16:33, Christ says, "In this world you will have tribulation; but be of good cheer, I have overcome the world." If the son of God Himself says we will have trouble in this life, why should we expect something different? He uses both smooth times and adversity as teaching tools to lead us to the specific place where He wants us so we can ultimately be blessed. If we only experienced good times and never went through hardships, there would really be no reason to bless us because our lives would be in a perfect state of being. We would not want or lack for anything.

Adversities are a direct ticket to a blessing. Of course, there are those times when we get into trouble, then pray for a magic carpet to appear to neatly sweep our mess under the rug. There are always consequences for sin, which we bring upon ourselves. Sin keeps us away from the abundant life Christ wants us to have. There is one more thing worth noting about Job before we derail this train of thought. The

Bible says Job used a potsherd, which is a piece of sharp, broken pottery and scraped his sores while he sat in the midst of the ashes. In Job's days, ashes were a sign of mourning. People would put ashes on their head or face to show they were in sorrow or mourning. I believe when Job sat down amongst the ashes, he was not only in mourning because of the great pain he was suffering, but also because he was confused and exasperated. It truly was a time of "ashes to ashes, dust to dust," for Job. He must have asked several times what purpose the suffering would serve in his life. Nevertheless, if you read a book as I sometimes like to do— speed read through the beginning and skim the middle to quickly get to the happily ever after ending—we see that the Lord blessed the latter days of Job much more than his beginning. There is a very interesting and comforting ending to Job's story. When I read the whole book, I saw it does not end the way I assumed it would. During Job's turmoil, he had a grand, ole' pity party with a few of his good friends. They all questioned the reason God had made or allowed Job to go through so much pain and suffering. However, Job must have handled his painful crisis in a way that was pleasing to God, because halfway through the eighth verse in the forty-second chapter, God said, "and my servant Job shall pray for you. For I will accept him (Job), least I deal with you (Job's friends) according to your folly; because you have not spoken of me what is right, as my servant Job has."

From this ending, we can gather that it is perfectly

acceptable to mourn and ask God why. It's even permissible to be upset over your circumstances and to wish you were not alive. Job cursed the day he was born, but in the end, God gave him double for his trouble. Even when Job could do nothing but watch his world go up in flames, spend time sitting in the ashes, and mourn over his losses and pain, he never denied God's presence or wisdom throughout the crisis. This provided God with an avenue in which He could richly bless Job because he pleased God with his words, as well as his actions, whereas Job's friends did not.

I truly wish I could claim that I gave God an easy street which he could use to pour blessings down on me, but I'm afraid that was far from the case. I was having my own grand pity party, however unlike Job's, mine was destructive. I lashed out at everyone and everything, including myself. I felt so alone and angry because I had to stop the life I had known and begin anew with yet another assistant. Right or wrong, I vowed to never again get close to another personal assistant. It was like the scene from *Gone with The Wind* where Scarlet O'Hara picks up a big dirt clod and vows never to be hungry again, God as her witness. The vow was more practical and sounded much better coming out of her mouth than it did mine.

Have you ever noticed how similar the words "abundant" and "abandon" look? Only two letters separate them. Not only do they look similar, but they can feel very similar too. When Amanda left, I felt empty, hopeless and angry. Even though I was happy she was going to spend every day with the love of her life, I felt incredibly angry and left out in the cold. I did finally get up off the floor (with mom's help) and faced the fact that I would have to soon start all over with someone new.

Once again, it was time to test the waters with the infamous ad. Since I wasn't going to school or working, it wasn't as critical to find a personal assistant right away. That was both good and bad. Good because there wasn't an urgent need to find someone to fit into my life's schedule because my life had totally changed since graduation. On the opposite end, because my life had totally changed, I felt as though my future was entirely out of my hands. Being the control freak I was in those days, the feeling was not good for anyone concerned.

A very sweet woman named Annie helped me out during my extended stay with my folks, however because of my vow, I was about as easy as a cactus in bloom to get along with. My stay at my parents' place turned into the three hour tour of Gilligan's Island. Thank goodness mom and dad's "island" was a much more hospitable place than the one on *Survivor*. Even though mom, dad, my sister and Annie did everything to make me feel at home, I refused to let that feeling of warm acceptance infuse my soul and confuse me. I was on a mission to be miserable and did an outstanding, or in my case, out-sitting job.

When an old school chum of dad's said he had a deal for me, I was all ears. Darvey was a rehabilitation counselor and told me about a place where I could live without a personal assistant and get a master's degree. I immediately thought he must have been Moses reincarnated and packed my bags ready to follow him faithfully into the wilderness. And believe me, living in an independent living facility was the wilderness compared to life as I had known it.

The time I spent at Independence Manor was wonderful, wild, and full of challenges. I faced daily tests such as managing three part-time personal assistants. I was entirely responsible for making my own schedule so I had to ensure one of the assistants showed up by 6:00 a.m. so I could catch the van to school by 7:30 a.m. If one of my assistants was sick, I had to schedule a back-up to come and help me get on with my day. Going to the bathroom and eating was never a spontaneous decision. It always entailed strategic planning for one of my assistants to meet me on campus or work at those critical times. Although evenings were a bit more relaxed, it still meant guaranteeing someone was there before and after dinner to help do chores around my place. God forbid if I had a night class or a meeting after hours of the van runs, because it totally threw our routine into a tizzy. I would have to find a willing participant to drive me there, stick around, and take me back home. Some might say I traded one adventure for three or more migraines by moving out on my own. Those were some of the most stressful days I've ever faced, but I would never trade the experience for anything in this world.

As I rolled onto the van lift the first morning of summer

school, it felt as though someone had sucker punched me in the stomach. As much as I had longed and prayed for a sweet taste of independence, absolutely nothing in life prepared me for looking into my mom's teary eyes to say good-bye. All of the collected memories and bad feelings I had neatly bottled up from tedious arguments between mom and me about my independence didn't spit on the fire that was stoking deep within.

On the nine-hour journey to my new home, I mentally rehearsed my big, farewell speech many times. I was determined to gain momentous strength by dwelling on how often mom had told me the move was totally irrational because I could never live by myself, versus the number of times dad and my close friends said, "You can do it." But all of my determination instantly dwindled as I looked into my parents' eyes, brimming with tears and said the last good-bye before heading off to my new, independent life. Echoes of conversation between us from the night before flooded my thoughts like tidal waves. The walls in my apartment at Independence Manor were so thin, they appeared to indeed talk. Eavesdropping was a popular sport there. Privacy was an unheard-of commodity. This worked as both an asset and a liability for the people who lived there, because if one needed help, help was practically just a shout away. But if you wanted some privacy or wanted a late-night jamming session with friends, you were certain to have a "jamming" session with Gracie, the apartment manager, the next day. Thank goodness, Gracie's heart was full of grace with the eyes of an angel because she saw the best in everyone, including me. I'll never forget the words that flowed out of mom's mouth the night before they left me in this "brave new world." The last thing I do each night before laying down is connect my electric wheelchair to the battery charger. It did not take long to discover that if I wanted to move the next day, I had to plug it in every night. But at that time, I was not accustomed to the process of charging my chair because dad, mom, or my personal assistant had always done it for me. It wasn't because the task was too difficult or beneath me. It was just easier for them to do it because they could match up the plug fittings much faster than I could. My coordination is the pits and by the end of the day, I was usually too tired to exert the amount of energy it would take to do it. After a day of moving and running errands in a new town, my nerves were shot and my aim was way off. My mom was not lying when she anxiously exclaimed to dad, "It took Jonean thirty minutes last night to plug in her chair. How in heavens is she going to make it through a day on her own?"

I said goodbye to my parents the next day. The farewell speech I had rehearsed quickly disintegrated under my hot tears. It was one of those rare moments where I did not open my mouth for fear I would have an emotional eruption on the spot. Determined not to be the new kid on the van who cried the first day of school, I faked a smile and said "Love ya," and quickly got locked into place in the van. Bruce, the driver, asked if I was okay, seeing that I was fighting back tears through my smile. I don't know which was worse, his kind but stupid question, or seeing mom and dad follow our van until they had to turn off.

For a few moments, I seriously considered bailing out at the next corner, flagging down my parents' car, and saying, "April fools!" But I didn't because I didn't want to appear to be a bigger wimp than I already seemed. I drew a deep breath and reminded myself that my dream of independent living was coming true. At that point though, I wasn't sure if it was a good dream or a bad one. All I really knew was that I was determined to prove I could master both a master's degree *and* living on my own.

Bruce, the short, burly driver, had several years of experience driving the van, so he was quite adept at unfastening wheelchair tie downs, quickly rolling his passengers onto the lift, and swiftly lowering them down onto the sidewalk at their destination. Many had warned me that he was about as friendly as a mad porcupine, but I found a soft "Pillsbury dough" side within him. He kept up a gruff, Napoleon demeanor to keep people at arm's length in order not to be used or hurt, but I saw through this façade the first day he dropped me off at school. I tried to calmly ask him when and where he wanted to pick me up. As Bruce tried to tell me where he was picking up passengers on campus that day, he could see the increasingly frantic look in my eyes because I had no clue where anything was, other than my class and the bookstore. With a halfway exasperated sigh, he caved in and said, "Never mind, forget it. I'll pick you up here at Birdwell at 11:45, okay?" Then he got into the van and drove off.

Exhilaration. That's the feeling that lingered with me all day. I was doing simple, but important tasks I had never done before, such as maneuvering to class by myself. Pine trees and grass never looked as crisp and green as they did that morning. Even though the air was warm and heavy, the sweet aroma burst through to all of my senses. It was a moment when I could do nothing but thank God that I was there and beg Him to stick close to me from then on. After that moment of awe, I headed to my Traumatic Brain Injury class. I was a little nervous about getting situated in the right place and meeting my assigned note-taker, so I allowed a fifteen-minute margin of error. Not only did I make it through the day with flying colors, I also excelled in the class. I either identified with or knew someone who had every symptom described in the book! A wave of relief rushed over me when I saw Bruce drive up to take me home. Home? What was this new place I called home? It struck me as odd that the place I called home three days ago was totally different from the place that was home now. Gracie met me with a big, welcoming smile as Bruce unloaded me from the van.

"Hi, how did it go," she asked in her *sweet*, East Texas twang.

"Great, great, they haven't kicked me out yet," I replied.

Her beautiful, brown, tiger eyes sparkled as she laughed

and exclaimed, "Well, that's always a good sign after the first day."

After light chit-chat, she told me I was always welcome to come to the local hang-out, better known as her office, anytime. It's a good thing her offer was legitimate because I took her up on it often! Another big wave of relief washed over me when I beheld Cora, my second personal assistant; a spunky, china doll, drive up to feed me lunch. The day we met, I thought there was no way a petite five foot one woman could handle the job of taking care of me. Boy, was I wrong! When I watched her cook up a storm in my three by three kitchenette, I knew we would become fast friends. And we did! We spent many Friday nights over a few quarts of Ben & Jerry's ice cream conducting major gripe sessions about life. Cora, about her cute, rebel boyfriend Roy, and me, about the ridiculous requirements of graduate school. Time flew by, as it always did when Cora came. We ate lunch and before I knew it, it was time for her to go to her afternoon class. It was difficult to look cool while saying goodbye, and at the same time holding on to her hand with a death grip, double checking when she was scheduled to come back. After reassuring me with that devilish grin of hers that she would be back that evening, she made a mad dash out the door.

For the first time, I was alone in my own apartment. As much as I had dreamed of this moment, I wasn't sure how I felt about it. That exhilarating feeling of independence was still beating wildly within me, but an eerie feeling of aloneness loomed about like a shadow. I thought about calling Amanda, but I didn't know what to say. Bragging seemed to be a bit premature because I had yet to conquer a night alone, but I wanted to share this strange, new sense of autonomy with her. It was so mysteriously magical that I was at a loss for words.

Although I have lived with cerebral palsy all my life and gone to special-ed classes with other people of various disabilities, up until that time, I had never actually lived around other people with disabilities. However, living with people with disabilities versus just going to school or occasionally socializing with them opened my eyes to a whole new world. The first day I entered Gracie's office and met a few of my neighbors, I knew I was in for a treat! Gracie flung open the door and invitingly said, "Come on in and chew the fat with us." I instantly felt welcomed by her but wasn't sure about the vibe from the other two guys in the room. Harry and Gil turned out to be some of the nicest gentlemen in the complex, but at that time, the way they looked me over made me feel like a piece of delectable fat on prime rib au jus.

It's a toss-up as to whether my horizons were broadened from receiving a master's degree, or from my time at Independence Manor. There were people living with physical and emotional pains so deep, I wondered how they still existed. Take, for instance, Harry. Harry was indeed hairy. He had a long, gray ponytail and a full, gray, unkempt beard that roughly resembled a sea captain's. His language roughly resembled an old sea dog's too. An unsightly yellow circle permanently outlined his mouth from years of chain smoking. Harry's story was unfortunately not unlike many other valiant vets. He served in Vietnam as one person and returned home a very different man. The changes were primarily due to a head injury and other health issues. People said Harry had a bad temper and chased his family and friends away, but fortunately, I never saw that side of him. All he ever showed me was his jovial, damaged side. I was grateful because I had a gut feeling he could have been quite unreasonable and mean with the right amount of alcohol in his system. Gil, on the other hand, was on the other end of the spectrum. He was a relatively young, brooding, good-looking country boy with a ten-foot tall chip on his shoulder. His unpleasant attitude was primarily due to the way he became disabled. It was a freak accident that unfortunately sometimes happens when adolescents recklessly horse around. While in high school, Gil and his friends were rough housing in a lake one sunny day when he slipped on a rock, broke his neck, and subsequently became a paraplegic. Gil was perfectly fine just as he was considering all that he had been through, but I took it as my personal mission to knock that huge chip off his shoulder and endow him with a better attitude. We rarely saw eye to eye on anything. Gil was his own man, nothing more, nothing less. Despite all my "helpful" advice, I did not exactly succeed in helping him gain a more positive perspective. But I did chisel away at some of his block-headed, male, chauvinistic ideas. Some said Gil and I were like oil and vinegar. They also claimed that as volatile as our friendship was, we must be brother and sister, or destined to be together. Fortunately, neither speculation was true. As stubborn as we both were, one of us would surely be dead by now. After getting to know Gil's defeatist outlook a bit, I thought the nicest thing about him was his black Labrador service dog, Shady. I truly felt sorry for her because not only did Shady have to live with Gil, she was also his constant coworker.

Gil was not only Gracie's assistant manager and "watch dog" on the weekends, but he was also blessed with a green thumb, so he did the landscaping too. The grounds of Independence Manor were always colorful and immaculate, thanks to those two. Gil primarily relied on Shady's loyalty and sure footing to get here, there, and everywhere on the complex since he did not have a motorized device to get around. Even though he was a good "daddy" and never abused or neglected Shady, I always thought she deserved a lot more rewards for lugging him around all day.

Before I knew it, it was five o'clock and time for Gracie to go home. We dispersed our interesting little soiree and went to our pleasant, but quiet abodes. Cora came back at six just as she said she would to finish out the day with a great dinner and lively conversation. After preparing me to kick back for the night, she left and I was alone again. It hit me that this was going to be my life from now on. A smile washed over me as I remembered all of the things I imagined I would do on my first night of total freedom. Instead of doing any of the nutty, celebratory things I had envisioned for that pivotal night in my life, I concerned myself with the domestic, practical stuff, like locking my door correctly and ensuring safe landing in my bed without falling on some vital part of my body. Seeing that the door lock did indeed work after the third check, I watched television. It was soothing in an odd way because it was the only consistent thing in my place at that time that reminded me of my old home. I was too sensitive to my new surroundings to get engrossed in a program. After listening to the echo of mom's concerns in my mind, and wondering just how much of an adventure charging my chair would be, I decided to face my Goliath. It only took me fifteen minutes to plug in my chair correctly.

As I swung my legs into bed and snuggled under the covers, a feeling of accomplishment and pride coursed through my body as I realized it only took *half* the time it took the night before. It's funny how accomplishing new tasks independently can mean so much. I closed my eyes and tried to shut my ears to the sounds of my new home. Eventually, sleep caught up with my racing mind and forced it to surrender. I'll never forget the question my professor asked me the next morning as I sped into class. With a twinkle in his eye, he said, "Well, Miss Walton, how was your first night alone?" Professionals say the first answer that pops into your head is always the correct answer. I would have to say that my answer was indicative of my whole stay at

Independence Manor. With an effortless grin, I exclaimed. "It was wonderful! I think?"

Chapter 6
1992–1994

God knew I needed a friend.

You have probably seen the beautiful print of a little boy and his dog with the caption underneath that says, *God knew I needed a friend, so he sent me you.* It's full of vivid colors that overwhelm your senses with goodness and light. That is the feeling I had when I came to know Zoey, my neighbor. I had successfully completed the second summer term and had a few days before the fall semester began, which meant I had more time to wander about in my new environment. Most of the people around me had lived at Independence Manor for years and were content with the ways they filled their lives. Though I met an overflow of very nice neighbors, there was no one I meshed with. Our different backgrounds were as varied as the reasons we were there. But thanks to Gracie, things were about to change.

I have no doubt that what I am about to say will offend most of you (at least I hope it does). Nevertheless, my gut reaction when I saw Zoey was, "Oh my, what in the world will I ever have in common with this severely immobile person?" Thinking back now, it pierces my heart that I was so ignorant and gutless. It also strikes me as terribly ironic, given that most people undoubtedly have the same initial reaction towards me. In fact, some have probably had worse reactions considering my spastic limbs and the fact that I am known to speak in unknown tongues. While people don't mean to, their facial expressions are a dead giveaway to their thoughts. "Who let the traveling freak show in?" At first glance, Zoey's appearance was a bit overwhelming because her chair was big and bulky to support all of the technologically advanced features on it. She was paralyzed from the neck down so she controlled her electric wheelchair with a chin device. Her arms and legs were lifeless weights; quite the opposite of her heart and brain. The name Zoey in Greek means "life." How to live life to the fullest is exactly what she showed me how to do. Once I got past the exterior, I found two huge, mystic, oceanic, blue-green eyes that captured my attention right away. Her long, luscious, dark eyelashes were such a contrast to her gorgeous eyes. Her cheeks and lips were something I was jealous of because they had a remarkable rosy glow all year round.

I'll never forget watching Zoey zip past my window headed to her apartment. She had a wild-eyed, apprehensive, determined look on her face reminiscent of how my face probably looked the day I made the big move to Independence Manor. I chuckled and hoped she'd had more luck processing her feelings than I did. Believe it or not, we were both too shy to make the first move so we let Gracie do the introductions. I saw Gracie and Zoey talking outside my window a few days after she moved in, so like a nosey neighbor, I barged out my door to say, "Hey, what's going on?"

Gracie said, "Zoey, meet your neighbor, Jonean. Jonean, Zoey."

With bashful confidence, we both said hi. As you have probably figured out by now, I am not shy for long. I showed more restraint than Samantha's nosey neighbor, Gladys Kravitz, on the sitcom *Bewitched*. Instead, I found myself looking for opportunities to get together to soak in the comfort we instinctively gave one another. Sometimes when a person has lived with a disability for a long time, especially a severe one, it's easy to fall into the mind trap of looking at able-bodied friends through the lens of a "what- have-you-done-for-me-lately-I-need" kind of attitude. Most of the time, it's not to intentionally make the able-bodied person feel guilty about not being disabled, it's because our physical needs are so great and our capabilities so limited, it's hard not to look for, and prefer, a friend who can provide the physical, mental and emotional support we need. The problem with this mindset is we tend to overlook or negate the friend that's right in front of our faces because we're too busy searching for a "better" friend. Though it seems like an elementary lesson I should have learned a long time ago, Zoey taught me this. There were times when we could give each other nothing, except a smile and a good ear. Most days, that's all we really needed.

When I was going to my counseling classes, there were a few canned questions they taught us that were supposed to help us gain insight when interviewing clients. I don't mean to make light of the academic world, but some of those questions sounded ridiculous. I was embarrassed for them to come out of my mouth. The question, "And how did that make you feel?" ranked high among our favorites. When Zo or I had a bad day, we would glare at each other and ask that stupid question, "And how does that make you feel?" For special effect, I would cross my eyes and legs when asking this award-winning question.

One particularly hot, East Texas summer day, our favorite question proved to be preposterous. The day started off sticky and ended even stickier. I got up at my usual time, around 6:30 a.m. to turn on the coffee pot before my assistant showed up at 6:45 a.m. My level of anxiety arose with every minute as 6:45 came and went. 7:00 a.m. ticked by and I was still in my pajamas with no coffee in me. So, I did what any true coffee addict would do. I took the coffee pot off the burner and put it in the refrigerator to cool while I dressed for class. I found some clothes that looked decent and fairly easy to put on and primped for a minute to ensure that I would not scare anyone. Afterwards, I rolled back into the kitchen, stuck a straw in my cooled off coffee and sucked it down before heading off to school with the help of Bruce.

The rest of the day seemed to have a nice ebb and flow to it in spite of the hectic, self-powered start. That is, until I discovered that my bank card was not in my wallet. I went home and tore my place apart thinking it probably fell out of my bag. After a few hours of frantic searching with no luck, I made two panicked phone calls. The first was to the bank to report and cancel my missing card. The next was to report this out of body and mind experience to my parents. As if all of this weren't bad enough, my parents informed me that a large deposit had been made on the card a few days prior. This was the only time I was truly sorry that my dad was a gracious giver because it meant some thief was the recipient of a month's worth of living expenses, and not me. I went through all of the proper hoopla at the bank and police station to file charges against the crook, but to add insult to injury, the surveillance camera was malfunctioning that day so they weren't able to catch a glimpse of the culprit. At that point, I really didn't know whether to laugh hysterically or cry. I did both. My mind immediately jumped to the well-worn track in my mind that reminded me "This is not how it's supposed to be." Consequently, when Zoey asked me the infamous question, "And how does that make you feel?" it took all I had not to knock her out.

Though Zo, at the young age of twenty-six, had a jump start on me by four and a half years at this independent living thing, we were very much in the same boat, riding the same tumultuous waves. The challenges of acquiring and managing dependable assistants, while trying to make good grades in college often seemed an overwhelming task. Texas Rehab Commission required a 3.0 grade point average or higher. Since Zoey and I were both receiving funding from the agency, the incentive to study was much more compelling than "must-see TV." When we studied, we crammed hard. When we had the chance to play, we partied hard. It seems as if some of our favorite assistants came along soon after we moved in. BeBe was one of Zoey's main helpers and quickly became one of our favorites. In fact, sometimes BeBe did double duty and helped me out too. When she smiled or laughed, you couldn't help but laugh too. Her jolly, hazel eyes beamed with contagious joy that was much needed. She called her five four, bubbly body, "fluffy." Since Zo and I were her senior by several years, we felt it was our duty and honor to usher her into her twenty-first year in style. Our fly in the ointment was transportation. Neither of us had a van with a lift on it, so our choices of where to take BeBe were limited. We put our two heads together, along with two more heads, and got a room full of screaming young women. It just so happened that Kat, one of my all-time favorite assistants and friends was a music/drama major and had a good friend who was a male dancer. He graciously agreed to be our private dancer with one stipulation: we could not come to him. He would come to us.

His beautiful, shoulder-length, light brown hair, teasing hazel eyes, and tight twenty-something year old physique made him look like the perfect Tarzan. Our theme for the evening was, "Welcome to the jungle, Bebe!" His limber, boyish gyrations certainly sent a rumble throughout our "jungle!" In all my thirty-one years, I had never seen anyone turn as red or burrow their face so deeply in a pillow without suffocating as Bebe did that night. It was a very memorable birthday for everyone, even those who were not there, as I found out the following Monday. Gracie questioned why so many cars were at mine and Zo's place over the weekend. I never had proof, but my suspicion tells me Gil gleefully ratted us out. He was a party pooper and took great delight anytime he had something on either of us. With a deer in the headlights look and some not so quick thinking I said, "Well, some girls came over and you know, girls just want to have fun!" I don't know why, but from then on, when something was amiss at Independence Manor, Gracie came to us and asked, "So did you girls have some fun last night?"

In a whirlwind of spectacular autumn colors, fall blew in. Watching the trees change colors in the forest from my front yard and breathing in the crisp fall air brought an invigorating spark to my soul. Halloween was sweeping in with all of its festivities and Gracie hosted the annual spook party for the tenants of Independence Manor. I didn't want to go against the reputation I was making for myself, so I wore a rubber egg head mask and adorned my body in white trash bags and went as a cracked egg. Zoey went as a disabled woman. We both won. One for most realistic costume, and the other, best costume. Thinking about it now, I'm not sure how to take that!

The party ended at a reasonable hour and most sensible people were ready to retire for the evening. Since Zoey and I weren't sensible people, we weren't ready for the night to end. A few wine coolers magically appeared in my refrigerator, so I invited Zo over for a nightcap. At first she was skeptical of my ability to get the bottles out, opened, and into our mouths. So I said with a gleam in my eye, "Trust me babe. I've been doing this since high school!" Then I told her about the infamous wine story. Surprisingly, Zo became even more skeptical about my ability and informed me she would really prefer I get the drink into her mouth and not on her lap. After successfully opening the bottle, in spite of my spastic, shaking hands, I stuck a straw in the wine cooler, and up to Zo's lips without spilling much on her. She hated to brag on me, but she had to admit I was indeed talented. I placed the bottle in her lap and propped it up against her stomach with a long straw so she could take a sip whenever she wanted and I did the same. While enjoying our drinks, we discussed further entertainment possibilities for the rest of the evening. We debated watching a movie, but decided against it since Zoey's assistant was coming in an hour to help her into bed. Like a bad penny, Gil's name came up. As I've said before, the only thing wrong with him was that he was immovably his own man and not what I thought he could be. Zo always managed to see the better side of him, which frustrated the heck out of me because she was usually right. As much as I hated to disrupt our enlightening conversation, nature called and it was imperative that I answer. Looking at the toilet paper, I had a sudden epiphany about Gil—not that he reminded me of toilet paper—on the contrary. Halloween and wrapping houses have always gone together back home. I bolted out of the bathroom and excitedly told Zo my bright idea. "Oh girl," she said, "you've been smoking in the bathroom or your drink must be much stronger than mine! We can't wrap Gil's whole apartment or his tree!"

"I know, I know. But wouldn't it be funny if Gil got up to find his prized roses and flowers covered in toilet paper?" I said.

"I don't know. It's risky and kind of mean. But it would be funny to see his face. He'll be madder than the Mad Hatter! Give me another cooler for courage and we just may try it," Zo said with a grin.

About that time, our victim-accomplice, better known as Trista, Zoey's assistant, came to my place looking for her. We must have looked as mischievous as two Cheshire cats. Trista was young and just out of high school but far from naive. She was tanned, tall, and big boned which gave the impression that she was older than she was, and worked to her advantage in most cases. Her curvy frame was accompanied by a boisterous east Texas drawl. She was country through and through and had a good heart.

"Oh no you don't, Gil will have mine and y'all's heads when he finds out who did it. Uh-uh, no way!" Trista exclaimed.

"Come on, you know you want to! Remember the rude remark he made that got your panties in a wad the other day. That one about where women belonged," Zo primed the pump.

"Ya know it would be kind of funny to give that ol' wet booster something to crow about. Okay I'm in, but I ain't taking no blame for it. It was y'all's whiskey bright idea," Trista slyly said with a smirk.

I dashed to the bathroom and showed Trista where the goods were kept. Too bad we didn't have outrageous sombreros to go with our ensemble, but that didn't stop us from charging out the door like The Three Amigos. We were on a mission! Looking back, I truly don't know what we were thinking, or if we were thinking at all because a number of things could have really gone bad. A good, country boy like Gil could have had a gun by his bed and used us for target practice, or he could have told Shady to attack us. Not to mention the trespassing charges Gil could have slapped on us. He would have enjoyed a hearty laugh if Zo and I would have had to call Gracie to put up bail for vandalizing some plants at Independence Manor. As obvious as it would have been to any thinking person, it's almost impossible to be stealth-like in an electric wheelchair. I'm truly amazed that Gil, Shady, or any of the neighbors never stuck their head out to see what was going on. All was eerily silent except for the hurriedly tip-toe sound of Trista's feet as she ran around Gil's small flower bed while I held the end of the roll. She created a nice weave of white that encircled the bushes, then laid the rest on the ground. Fighting back the giggles and constantly looking over our shoulders on the way back home proved to be almost an impossible feat. We all ran into each other hustling to get into my door without leaving a trace behind. Bets were made as to when our crime would be reported to Gracie. We had a mini swearing in ceremony similar to the girls in the YaYa Sisterhood, that we would never tell a soul of that evening's events.

Strangely enough, the next morning, the previous night's activities didn't seem like such a good idea. Both Zoey and I were on pins and needles, trying hard to deflect any attention that might come our way. Several days passed without word of our crime scene at Gil's. Our tension was through the roof. We thought about admitting our guilt but were hoping against all odds that Gil would let it lie. A few more days passed and everything seemed to be flowing along at a regular pace. Zo and I thought it was kind of weird that Gracie and Gil were looking at our tires, but not a word was said. Unbeknownst to me, they had devised a new tracking system and the track on my tires seemed to match the tracks that were unfortunately left at the very edge of Gil's flowerbed.

Shall we say, I was tracked down and busted! Once again, Gracie, wearing a big grin, posed the question, "So, on the evening of October 31, 1993, did you girls have some fun?" With an interesting combination of a deer in the head lights daze, and a sheepish grin, I stuck my head out of Gracie's office door and exclaimed "Zoey, you've got some s'plaining to do!" Thank goodness Gracie was, as always, true to her name, full of grace, and saw more humor in our silly, juvenile prank than Gil did and didn't boot us off the property.

Discovery can be a good or a bad thing as it relates to self-discovery. That fun, but infamous evening, when we had drinks at my place made me aware of how easy it is to escape from the reality of life behind a bottle of booze. Not that I particularly needed to escape from anyone or anywhere at that time. I felt as if I was right where I needed to be, on my own and going to school. But alcohol seemed to be the only thing that made me feel as if life was indeed what it's supposed to be. That tornado of self-doubt and emptiness did not touch down nearly as often with booze. It took away my blues temporarily and leveled the playing field in the great game of life. It numbed all of the what-ifs and made the "what is" feel manageable. Drawing outside of my comfort zone didn't feel so abstract. My logic was if a little alcohol could make everything well with my soul, imagine what a lot would do?

* * *

Instead of the YaYa Sisterhood, Zo and I formed an elite entity, the Vacuum Club. I'm not proud of it now, but the simple rules for becoming a part of the club amounted to how quickly someone could suck down a beer through a straw. If someone we invited over could keep up, or beat Zo's or my record, they were in. Of course, Zoey and I held the top noble titles of "Eureka" and "Hoover" respectively, while those who joined the Vacuum Club were given lower ranking titles like "Dust Buster" or "Dirt Devil." To add to our authenticity, we had forest green t-shirts with our titles proudly monogrammed in white on the left side. As ridiculous and unhealthy as this "club" was, it confirmed a few suspicions about myself that I had already assumed. I liked being needed. I enjoyed being the drink opener and counselor. For the first time in life, I was on the giving, rather than the receiving, end and it felt good. I took great delight in solving people's problems or helping them see the lighter side of life through humor.

King Solomon was ever so wise when he wrote this in Proverbs 15:13, "A merry heart makes a cheerful countenance but by sorrow of the heart the spirit is broken." Looking back on those experiences, I understand that hurt people have an innate desire to help other hurt people. In fact, many go into human services or personal assistant fields for this very reason. We feel that because "we are there" or "have been there," we have the right stuff to help others avoid the pitfalls we've stumbled into. At first glance, it seems like a logical win-win situation. It makes sense to be more receptive to someone with similar experiences. Unfortunately, people have a hard time following rules. Two negative people rarely make a positive outcome. The negativity of one person usually overshadows or rubs off on the other and contaminates the relationship, whether personally or professionally. Helping others can be addictive because it makes us feel as if our own wounds are being healed. But at the same time, we must be conscientious not to unload our old baggage onto the one we are trying to help.

While I was working on my master's degree and thereafter, it never seemed to fail that I would have at least one personal assistant who had many, many more problems than I ever imagined. Albeit, their problems were not as visible as mine, but there were times when their emotional and mental baggage exceeded my weight limit. As much as I enjoyed helping them, it became too heavy a burden to bear. In any relationship there is going to be a certain amount of give and take but sometimes I wanted to tell people what May Ellis told her new assistant in the movie *Passion Fish*. "Chantelle, you got problems, personal problems, and I don't want to hear them."

I don't know how I kept my grades high enough to stay in good academic standing while also maintaining my outstanding membership in the Vacuum Club on the weekends and sometimes during the week, depending on my stress levels. My mom has often pointed out that during my college years, I was a pro at finding good excuses for anything that suited me. But as most students discover, the closer to the lambskin I got, the faster it felt as if I were chasing my own tail. This meant less time for extracurricular activities.

Eighteen months into my master's program, there was a terrifying hurdle that each counseling student had to jump over called Candidacy. It essentially consisted of being closed up in a four by six, stuffy office piled high with ungraded papers, and three professors asking students what counseling theory they concurred with the most. The whole process lasted approximately forty-five minutes from start to finish, but it felt like three scorching hot days had passed judging from the amount of sweat pouring off my body. One of the main purposes of the practice was to check to see if each student was truly a sound candidate for graduation. This not only included a blood, sweat, and tears investigation on how thorough our knowledge was on the theory we most agreed with, but also a brief review of our courses and grades to ensure we were on the right track. The story of my life suddenly flashed before my eyes as I beheld three professors poring over my transcript. They all seemed pleased with my grades and commended me but, it appeared they all came to a shocking realization that had not occurred to them before. Although those professors talked with me almost daily for nearly two years and were aware of my speech and other limitations, I had the distinct, uncomfortable feeling that the faculty really didn't expect me to complete the program. In unison they said, "You're on schedule to graduate, but we are having trouble finding a place for you to complete your practicum and internship, due to your speech impediment. In order for us to feel comfortable in placing you and for you to successfully complete our requirements, we are going to train you to use a speech augmentation device called a Liberator. This only requires one more semester with us, to ensure you're fully competent before we place you into the real world."

Instead of reacting with an attitude of gratitude as I'm sure they had hoped for, I looked at them as if they were totally nuts. My hot, chili pepper temper got the best of me as I bit my tongue nearly in half and fought back the fiery urge to say, "So let me get this straight. You allowed me to get this far into the program, then tell me that I can't graduate with my good friends because you're afraid I'm more of a liability than the asset you've led me to believe I was for the last eighteen months?! You're doing this to cover your own behind in case of a lawsuit in the real world. And if I've been living in some fantasy world instead of the real one, boy have I been ripped off. If you saw this coming, why didn't you stop my progress earlier and give me the box? You think that a weird, computerized voiced encased in an ugly, reddish-orange bulky box can replace or supplement the voice I've worked on for thirty-two years?!"

These thoughts were like firecrackers exploding in my mind in rapid succession. When the fireworks finally ceased,

I managed to say, "Well okay. Thanks for your time," and wheeled out the door.

Bruce picked me up on time but it felt like he was an hour or more late. I had never completely put my heart and soul into anything as I had the past nineteen months and now I wondered what was the point. I was being punished for the thing I hated most about myself—my speech. Even in an accepting environment like the Rehabilitation Counseling Program and Independence Manor, it was still an issue. My personal demon tracked me down once again. The old adage, you can run but you cannot hide, proved true for me once again, only this time I felt like I had been hit with the velocity of an atomic bomb. Not only was my speech impediment a major embarrassment to me, it was going to hold me back from the very thing God had finally called me to do, or so I thought. Looking back, they were only asking for a five month delay towards graduation, but being the drama queen that I sometimes am, I mistakenly took it to mean I was not good enough to graduate with my peers. If I was truly fulfilling God's purpose for my life, how could He allow this set back? It never occurred to me this was the only way God could make me color outside the lines of the picture I had drawn in permanent ink. I was so hell-bent on serving God as the best counselor I could be, I did not want to consider that He might not have the same plans in mind. Isn't that part of an abundant life? You feel confident in directing your own steps until you find yourself face to face with a concrete wall or realizing that taking a U-turn is the only choice you have. A U-turn that seems inconvenient for us may be the detour God uses to get us to look at a different plan.

On the ride home, I began to think about a career as a nun. Maybe I could join a convent that required a vow of silence and allowed me to keep a vineyard for a winery. That would be the best of both worlds. No one would need to understand what I was saying and I could volunteer to be a taster. At least my experience in the Vacuum Club would be put to good use. At home, my mind went into retrospective mode and I spiraled down into that familiar, gloomy funnel that threatened to suck me in as I thought, "It's not supposed to be this way."

I called an emergency Vacuum Club meeting. I wanted to celebrate passing Candidacy and being so beloved by the faculty that they wanted to detain me for another wonderful semester that would primarily be focused on my speech impediments. As usual, Zoey and BeBe patiently listened to me rant and tried to show me the bright side of midnight. We reached the conclusion that I needed to get out more and not take academics so seriously, which sounded good to me.

*　*　*

The Nacogdoches fair and rodeo were coming to town. Gracie graciously gave us a ride to the festivities and this time, they were not leaving without me. It was

1993 and that year's headlining act was the then-rising star, Toby Keith. Unsurprisingly, Gracie had a high percentage of female riders that trip. We all wanted to gaze upon the hot, hunky, young cowboy. His song, *Should've Been A Cowboy*, was a hit that year so he graciously obliged his fans by singing it several times. As he sang, I couldn't help but think to myself, *I bet the cows could understand my ooooooo without the help of that stupid Liberator. Now that would be real liberating—earn a master's degree in counseling only to go counsel bovine.* Thank goodness Keith had not yet come out with another one of his hits, *How do you Like me now?* In the mental shape I was in, I probably would have pictured myself in a vineyard adorned in a habit, dancing around the Liberator. If I danced around fast enough in my habit, it would eventually make me airborne. Then I could be the new version of the Flying Nun. Needless to say, I gathered my thought and it turned out to be a sweet and memorable evening.

Zoey and I were decked out in our best western duds and if I may say, we got a few double takes from a few good looking cowboys, although I'm not sure whether their heads turned because they were dazzled by our beauty, or because they wanted a second gaze at our traveling circus. Zo and I sat by one another and laughed so much that people wondered what was in our cups. That's okay. We enjoyed keeping people wondering.

Reality came with the morning sun and reminded me I

had a paper due on Monday. Though my feelings were still a bit crushed and disgusted by the outcome of Candidacy, I was not insane. Keeping my grades up was still vital to my psyche so I spent my Saturday writing against the clock while Zo and friends went to the chili cook off at the fair. By now, Zoey had an old, blue cargo van so transportation on the weekends was not an issue as long as she could find a capable driver. The day went by at a reasonable pace considering my lack of enthusiasm and all that needed to be accomplished. Before I knew it, the sun began to set across the forest in my front yard. Trista and Zo were obviously having a good time because I didn't hear a peep from them through our shared, paper thin wall. All seemed well until Gracie called out of the blue. We usually tried not to bug her on weekends because her young family needed "Gracie time" too. I wasn't sure if it was good or bad when I heard her voice.

"Whatcha doing," Gracie asked.

"Homework. Is there anything more to my life?" I mused.

"Yes, yes, someday soon," she replied.

Sarcastically I asked, "Will I still be alive to see that day?"

"You'd better. Just thought you'd want to know Zo pulled one of her stunts this afternoon and is in the hospital. Won't be home tonight."

I hesitantly asked, "Should I be there?"

"Nah, unless you really want to go. It was the usual. Her engine just overheated. She ought to be home tomorrow or the next day. Trista's coming by to get a few of her things and will spend the night with her in the hospital."

"Okay, thanks. Please keep me posted. Tell her I love her. I'm praying for her."

"K. See ya Monday," Gracie gently said.

So much for an uneventful day. As hard as I tried to concentrate on writing, the stream had hit a concrete dam. I couldn't help but think how unfair Zoey's lot in life was. She had been very popular in school and was quite the athlete according to her. She was involved in her youth group and the local Fellowship of Christian Athletes. In fact, life as Zoey and her family had known abruptly stopped after a church youth trip when she unfortunately had an up close and personal experience with the bottom of a pool. Zoey would jokingly say it was because she tried to never do anything halfway.

Her spinal cord injury occurred in the neck area which classified her as a high-level quadriplegic. The higher the break or injury on the spine, the less control a person has over their body. The autonomic nervous system can even be damaged if the spine injury is high enough on the spinal column. Most of the time we never think about how much the autonomic system does until our respiratory system goes haywire and we're forced to deal with a life or death situation. In Zoey's case, the ability to perspire was null and void. Instead of perspiring, heat would build up and cause her core body temperature to rise to unsafe levels. Unfortunately, Zoey would overheat before she or anyone else would realize what was happening and that's what caused her to end up in the emergency room that weekend. She wound up staying in the hospital for five days. No matter how hard I tried to visit her that week, it was never the right time to catch a van ride. It was a long week for both of us, especially Zoey.

When she finally made it home, we tried to briefly make up for lost time, but knowing how much homework Zo had to catch up on, I thought it best to steer clear for a while until I was beckoned. And boy was I beckoned in a startling way. I've always dreamed of a good looking guy waiting for me outside my bedroom window. I guess that's why the chorus to Melissa Etheridge's hit song, *Come to My Window* was often my lullaby.

> *"Come to my window*
> *Crawl inside, wait by the light of the moon*
> *Come to my window I'll be home soon."*

In my groggy state, I thought, *Wow, it's finally happening.*
Tap. Tap. Tap.
"Ma'am wake up!"
Wait a minute, I thought, *what a nice guy. My prince has finally come.*
Tap. Tap. Tap.
Wait, is there really someone at my window. Oh, my gosh! I don't even have clean underwear on. What will mom say?
"Ma'am, wake up! Your neighbor told me to come get

you. She is in trouble. At that moment my heart started racing as my eyes bugged out. I was afraid I knew exactly what he was referring to.

"Okay, I am on my way!" I exclaimed.

I threw myself together as quickly as I could in my chair and opened my door carefully, to see if the young man was still outside. Much to my relief he was real and had disappeared as fast as he had appeared which caused me to wonder if I had dreamt the whole thing up. In case I hadn't, I hurried down the sidewalk to Zoey's place. I found her all wrapped up in her sheet from head to toe. This time she had panicked when she could not get the sheet off her face and hyperventilated, which made her overheat even more than the last time. I could not believe what I saw. I felt sick, because I had no clue she had been in so much trouble. The emergency cord in her room was just an ugly decoration by the bed because she couldn't reach up and pull it for help. I asked another award-winning stupid question.

"Are you okay, Zo?"

She gave one look that told me everything I needed to know and I immediately called BeBe. After I relayed the emergency to her, I went back to Zo and tried to cool her off by drenching her face with a cool washcloth. I turned on all the fans in hopes of taming the volcano boiling inside of her. As stupid as it was, I continually talked to her, praying to get some smart aleck reply, such as, "You are no Martha Stewart, so stop the act." Much to my disappointment I received only looks of panic. It felt like an eternity passed before BeBe showed up and called the ambulance.

Like a bad nightmare that haunts me, the look in Zo's eyes haunted me the whole day. By the end of the day, I had determined that there was something I could do to help. When I got home from school that afternoon, I swung by Gracie's office to get an update on Zoey's condition. Gracie assured me that she would be fine and at the same time, tried to break it to me gently that Zoey's folks no longer thought it was a good idea for her to live alone. Gracie was beginning to have her doubts as well about Zo's situation so she was at risk of losing her place at Independence Manor. After Gracie told me what I had feared all day, I exclaimed, "There has to be a better way! Zo can't go home. It's not time yet. Does Zo want to go?"

"Well no, not really. But...," Gracie tried to edge in.

"Okay, what about those new baby monitors advertised on TV. Do they really work"?

"Well I guess so, why?" Gracie asked.

I carefully chose my words this time. "Well, what if I got a set and put the receptor in my room so if Zo has any kind of trouble, I would hear her before it's too late. Then I'll call BeBe, Trista, you or 911 if I have to."

"You would do that? It's crazy you know, but it just might work." A slow grin appeared on her face.

That night, I called mom and in my heart, I fell on my knees. I was so moved by everything that had happened that day I just had to talk with her. I never in my entire life felt such a sense of responsibility and duty towards anyone as I did that day. It felt strange and scary. Thinking about the possibility that Zo could have died that morning gave me flashbacks to the stunts I've pulled against mom's better judgment, and I crumbled into a humble heap on the phone. All I could get out of my mouth was, "I'm so sorry mom for everything I've ever done. I never meant to hurt or scare you."

Of course, she inquired what I had done, and found it difficult to believe I was innocent for once. After a quick rundown of the day's events, she had the same reaction that Zo's mom did. She imagined the worst happening with me in charge. As usual, mom tried to talk me out of taking on this great responsibility. She finally gave up when I explained that she had helped make it possible to get my education. Now I wanted to help Zo get hers too.

The next day, we bought baby monitors and set them up in Zo's and my place. I highly anticipated Zoey's excitement about the monitors when she came home, but in true Zo fashion, she said, "What if I have guests?" My face dropped as I scrambled for a response.

"Well, I guess they will have to be smart enough to turn it off. That means you will have to come up with a higher standard of guests."

Speechless, Zo turned and rolled home. I am very glad to say Zo and I both made it through the rest of that semester without another heated situation. Because she had experienced such a rough go of it health and school wise, she decided to move home for a while and regroup. In 1996, Zo made the ultimate move and went home to be with the Lord. Each time I hear the song *Baby Blue* by George Strait, my mind trips back to our glory days. I'll always thank God for bringing us together for that special time because, as the song says, "She brought colors to my life that my eyes had never touched, and when she taught me how to care, I never cared so much."

Chapter 7
1995-1998

Not in Kansas anymore.

The biggest lie I told myself for years is that saying goodbye to loved ones gets easier with time. I thought I would be so excited to start my internship in Fort Worth, that leaving Independence Manor wouldn't make me sad.

It was a crisp, sunny, December morning. My dad had come to take me home for Christmas break and then on to Fort Worth, where I would start a brand-new adventure in the wonderful world of work. I always looked forward to the times Dad came to see me, but not that day. I dreaded it. His arrival meant the closing of a very precious chapter in my life. I tried everything I could to stay within the nice, neat lines I had proudly drawn for myself. There were no job openings where I could complete my internship working in Nacogdoches, so I begged Gracie to create a position for me at Independence Manor. Though Gracie was all for it and gave it her best shot, the board said no. As I rolled down the sidewalk of my humble, cracker box abode for the last time, it seemed as if a part of me was withering away like the trees in front of the house during winter. I was leaving with so much more than I came with.

As I approached the car, what I hoped for *and* dreaded came into view. Gracie, Gil, Bruce, Mercedes and several others gathered around for my big send-off. Some just came for proof of my departure so they could start their celebration. It was hard enough saying farewell to neighbors that I wasn't close to, but when it came to saying goodbye to Gil and Gracie, it was downright difficult. I slapped Gil on the back and thanked him for being the brother I never had. I also thanked him for the rotten times he had given me. He gave me one of his obnoxious, toothy grins and said, "Anytime."

Saving the hardest for last, I wheeled around and faced Gracie. I felt like I was living out the exact words of the song, *To Sir With Love.*

*"Those schoolgirl days of telling tales and biting nails are gone.
But in my mind I know they will still live on and on.
But how do you thank someone who has taken you from crayons
to perfume?
It isn't easy, but I'll try.*

*If you wanted the sky
I would write across the sky in letters That would soar a*

thousand feet high 'To Sir, With Love'

The time has come for closing books and long last looks must
end And as I leave I know that I am leaving my best friend
A friend who taught me right from wrong and weak from
strong That's a lot to learn, but what can I give you in return?"

Although I had rehearsed this moment a few times in my mind, when I looked into Gracie's noble, dark, tiger eyes as they brimmed with tears, I completely lost it. The eyes always got me. How could I possibly thank the one who had taken me from not being able to plug in my own chair in under thirty minutes, to taking responsibility for another's life, and all points in between? In my usual chicken fashion, I quickly hugged her, said thanks, and got in the car praying I could hold in the outburst that was threatening to erupt inside. Gracie, being the wise, precious person she was, had already prepared for our bittersweet moment, and stuffed into my hand the most precious letter I have ever received, hugged me, and said goodbye in her usual sweet, calm manner.

Despite the holidays resembling a "Hard Candy Christmas," as Dolly Parton sang about, Christmas with my family was wonderful. It flew by as fast as Santa making his rounds on Christmas Eve, and before I knew it, it was time to begin another adventure. I could not have picked a worse evening to move into the independent living facility in Fort Worth. It was raining and spitting sleet as the movers unloaded my precious cargo from the truck into another cracker box apartment. Dear ol' Dad claims my sisters and I take some kind of sinister delight in moving from place to place because every time we do, it is either a hundred and ten degrees above or twenty degrees below, and we never miss asking for his helping hand.

I should have taken heed of the weather that night. It was an ominous foreboding to my days there. I most certainly wasn't in Kansas anymore! People tried to warn me that all independent living facilities are different, but I had had such a great experience at Independence Manor, I couldn't fathom this new facility being worlds apart. But it was. It even felt different. The facility itself was newer and nicer than Independence Manor, but there always seemed to be a shady overcast. It possessed all of the modern conveniences of home. For instance, if I was ever in need of another "male dancer" to make a house call, all I had to do was go next door to a neighbor's apartment and ask to borrow her boyfriend for the evening. He was an alleged professional, but our "Tarzan" was much cuter. At least our dancer had all his pearly whites and a clear complexion. Another "convenience" that blew my mind was that if I was so inclined to do drugs, several neighbors could no doubt liberally supply me with my drug of choice. I know this for a fact because I caught one of my close neighbors with my personal assistant conducting a "business" deal in my bathroom one evening. I wasn't in Kansas anymore and I was suffering terrible withdrawals.

I felt like an outsider the entire eleven months I was there.

Not only was I a strong advocate of not frying one's brains out on drugs, I also worked for the Texas Rehab Agency, which had a strict stance against drug use. Since a large percentage of the residents were clients of the rehab facility, I was probably about as welcome as a voracious watchdog with fleas.

Thank the Lord, there was one sweet woman who befriended me. Sara, who was also received like a snobby outcast because she never smoked, rarely drank, had classical taste, and was goal-oriented. In other words, she was sweet but did not put up with much crap. Sara wore her gorgeous, blonde hair in a cute teddy bear haircut that softly framed her prim face and huge, dark chocolate eyes. Before her spinal injury, she was an extremely gifted musician in a metropolitan symphony orchestra. Hence, the classical taste. Though the accident robbed her physically and emotionally, her tenacious lioness spirit remained wholly intact. Sara drove daily to and from school in the maddening metroplex traffic, proving she could out-roar me any day. She was paralyzed from the midriff down, which meant she had much more control over her body than Zoey. She also had more control of her hands than I do and was a steady bottle opener for me. Her zippy, maroon Caravan was especially equipped to accommodate her needs and maximize her independent spirit. This worked for me because when an event came along worth venturing out *for*, we made it an adventure.

One such event was when Yanni, the Greek musician,

came to the metroplex for an outdoor concert, and we decided he was just too cute for us not to make the trip. Sara and I decided to go whole hog that evening and order our favorite, New York style pizza, before venturing out. While it wasn't the wisest of choices, considering the mess we made, I must say, it was mighty tasty.

After our feeding frenzy, we once again became Yanni-presentable with the help of a few towels and a lot of napkins. We couldn't have asked for a better evening. It was early May, and the air was beginning to have that soft, summer breeze feeling I love. Sara and I basked in wonderment as Yanni filled our senses to the brim with mesmerizing tunes and an intoxicating atmosphere. All seemed perfect until nature called. As hard as I tried to ignore the nagging call, it kept redialing. I had just gotten a jazzy new "Quickie p200" electric wheelchair and was bound and determined not to get a drop of anything on it. I squirmed until the last five songs, then got desperate. I leaned over to Sara and repeated a version of that commercial with the catchy jingle, "gotta go, gotta go, gotta go right now!" She laughed and made a snide comment about me having the impulse control of a five-year old. With considerable skill, we weaved our way in perfect bomber formation through the crowd to the restrooms. I bolted in ahead of Sara, praying for a handicapped stall that was not occupied by a non-handicapped person. Public businesses may claim to be accessible, however, that does not mean a wheelchair can easily be maneuvered in the stalls.

When I finally got in, the door wouldn't close. Considering my situation, there was no way I could pass on the opportunity for relief. Feeling very exposed to the world, I yelled at Sara, and asked her to pull off one of her best performances, and act like a door. Though she was unable to cover the whole doorway, I didn't feel quite as exposed. At work the next day, as I recalled the events of the previous night to my coworkers, they all teased me and said, "Now *that* is a prime example of the crip leading the crip."

I truly enjoyed working for Texas Rehab during my internship, but I hated the traffic. My place was only thirteen miles from the office, but it took anywhere from thirty to fifty-five minutes one way to get there. It was already hard enough to be timely with the help of the flaky assistant I had at the time. In hindsight, I experienced some of the same feelings as the monks who flog themselves to be cleansed of past sins. I didn't have any security while Bren was helping me because she was about as reliable as a one-armed monkey with a bad case of fleas performing brain surgery. Thank the good Lord, my bosses had mercy on my helplessness. They tucked me under their protective wings many mornings and drove all the way across the metroplex to give me a ride when Bren "forgot" to show up.

It's hard to say what I learned more from, the work itself or the world of office politics. I happened to be assigned to an office of eight strongly opinionated women, which was a good education in itself. In altruistic, graduate fashion, I made the grave mistake of reporting an incident involving a fellow employee and a vendor that could have been harmful to both my co-worker and the agency's reputation. To my naive amazement and embarrassment, instead of helping my co-worker out of a harmful situation, I was reprimanded for not minding my own beeswax. Then, suddenly that office couldn't afford, or find space, for another counselor. This unfortunate pothole in my career colored the rest of my time there as an intern and stalked me thereafter. There was no proof of it, but each time I applied for a new position in the agency, the same old story would rear its ugly head. I was qualified, but they preferred someone with more experience. If you're wondering how much use I got out of my fancy Liberator in the field, here's an idea. At each intake interview for the first month of my internship I gave people the choice of hearing my real voice or the robotic sounding box. Oddly, most of my clients had the same feelings towards the Liberator that I did because only three of approximately a hundred and thirty requested I use it. But who's counting?

Longing for more opportunity, anytime I got the chance to go to my old stomping grounds, I jumped on it. One Sunday shortly after my internship ended, Bailey happened to be preaching at a small church near Nacogdoches, so I decided to grace the congregation with my presence that morning. Through the years I had kept up with the adventures of Amanda, Bailey and their son, Brett, and vice-versa. One of the biggest adventures in their repertoire was the year they traveled across Texas in the evangelistic field. Bailey and Manda spent almost a whole year on the road, in a fifth wheel travel trailer when Brett was five years old. Now that's what I call adventurous and crazy! It's obvious by now that I would be crazy to expect anything less than a good time with Amanda and Bailey. Marriage had not tamed any of the nuttiness in either of them. If anything, they were even worse. Just like old times, something unusual would happen when we got together that would have us shaking our heads for years to come at the memories. The usual, witty banter between Bailey and I flowed as natural as breathing as we made our way to the small country church.

"Bailey, did you remember your sunglasses and tin cup? The congregation may enjoy your sermon much more if you sit in the corner and are mute. I may even donate a few bucks if you don't speak for a while!" I said as gingerly as I could.

"No, but I know after people hear the devil come out of your mouth, they'll be willing to give more if you leave the building. Heck, I would even throw in my paycheck if you leave, period," Bailey said with a huge smirk.

I asked as sincerely as I could, "Are you going to mention that you were once the poster child for cerebral palsy? You might get more sympathy for your preaching if you do!"

After church, we headed to Nacogdoches. I stuck my head out the window to savor the earthy smell of the East Texas piney forest along the way. As people with good taste do, we agreed to meet at the ice cream place on Main Street. The excitement of seeing Gracie and her two beautiful kids while eating ice cream was almost more than I could take. My theme song rose to a crescendo in my head, "Gotta go, gotta go, gotta go right now!" I asked to be excused before everyone arrived. Amanda kindly helped me get situated in one of the bigger stalls and all was right with the world once again. Realizing I had forgotten a bag in the van, I asked her to go and get it while I finished up. Manda quickly went, promising she would be right back. It is amazing how time flies when reading graffiti on the wall of a bathroom stall. You can learn some very interesting archeological trivia of the times. The old country song by Alan Jackson sums it up succinctly. You can find out "who's cheating who, and who's being true, and who don't even care anymore." It was so intriguing, I lost track of time. So, imagine the stunned look on my face when Amanda barged back in, looking like a wild-eyed Kramer in a Seinfeld episode.

"Oh! Thank the Lord you're here."

Stunned by her remark, I replied, "Of course I'm here. Where else did you expect me to be?!"

In a rush to get back and help me, Amanda hadn't paid attention to the bathroom sign, distinguishing male and female. As she called out my name, frantically looking in the stalls, and didn't see me, she thought I'd been kidnapped or taken up in the Rapture. She figured it was safe to assume no one would take me in the state I was in. Once she ruled out those possibilities, she realized she was not in the right bathroom and made a mad dash for the door. The horrifying mistake was verified when she walked out the door and saw the sign that read "women's room" across the hall. We exited the bathroom laughing hysterically. As we passed the sign, I pointed to it and said, "You might not be a redneck," but in the words of Jeff Foxworthy: "Here's your sign!"

* * *

The gut-wrenching day came when I found myself running out of time to find a job. I had conned Dad into paying three months' rent after my internship ended, in hopes of finding a counseling position in the metroplex. But, it just wasn't meant to be. It seemed like the harder I pounded the pavement, the more rejections I received. Winter was especially cold that year and I came down with pneumonia which, with my limited lung capacity, was awfully tough to beat. Mom and Dad put all four feet down and very strongly suggested I move home, at least for a while. Thank God my parents were okay with letting a piranha in their house, because I was about as lovable as one. I was so contagious with misery, people could catch it if they were within five feet of me. Counseling felt so right for me that I couldn't imagine how it could not feel right to God, too. How could He lead me so far in one direction only to slam the door and force me to take the one U-turn I promised myself I would never need to take?

Moving back in with my parents was the ultimate sign of defeat. I never wanted to be like other thirty-five-year olds who moved back in with mommy and daddy for various reasons. My tornado started churning and the thought that life was not supposed to be this way became my anthem. This time, the suction was so strong, it nearly destroyed me. I decided if I could not get a job in counseling, or the human services field, life had no purpose and was not worth living. It was a good thing I had cut back on my Vacuum Club consumption or else I might have sucked my way into heaven. I must admit, the thought did flash through my mind a few times. However, every time I drank too much, my gag reflexes would take over and shove me back into reality over the toilet or trash can. I am so grateful that God does indeed work in mysterious ways! To add insult to injury, Zoey's sudden passing during this transitional time weighed heavy on me. I never had a chance to say a proper goodbye. In my skewed thinking, I was not only mad at God for taking Zoey away before we had the opportunity to be old crips together, but, in a very selfish way, I was angry because He let Zo go home to be with Him rather than me. After all, it was me who was ready to end it all, not Zoey. Oh, don't get the wrong idea, I definitely grieved for her and for the loss of our closeness, but I could not help being envious that she would never again have to bother with the miseries of complete dependence on another person for life's necessities. Zo never again had to worry about whether someone would show up to feed her or be there when she got sick. She was free at last from all the bondages that so heavily burdened her in this short life, and I so desperately wanted to be free, too. Zo no longer had to fight the incongruence between the reality of her life, and what she thought it was supposed to be because, where she was, existence was perfect.

As I was whirled deeper and deeper into my tornado, I tried to justify Zo's untimely death. Zoey was unquestionably more sweet-natured than I ever tried to be. When it came to patience, she could out-wait me any day. Her inner strength was opposite of her outward shell. No wonder God called her home, and not me. I was not good enough to be in His presence. My thinking was skewed and screwed. I occasionally came up for a breath of fresh air, but I hung on tightly to this bottom rung of self-defeating thoughts for six years. During this period, I joined a national group that trained people on how to be effective advocates for disability issues. Their intense approach provided the perfect avenue to channel my frustrations. This cutting edge, policy-leading group strongly believed that the best way to learn something was by "just doing it."

One of the various projects we were assigned was an evaluation of the local services available for people with disabilities. So, I visited our Mental Health/Mental Retardation Center to see what types of services were available for their residents and non-residents. I must admit, my ulterior motive was to land a job. After interviewing Kamie, the director, for the hundredth time with the same, monotonous, run-of-the-mill questions, she looked over the rim of her glasses with her understanding, hazel eyes and asked if I happened to know a lady named Halie. She had worked at the Center about six years and currently was the activities director. Since Halie was from my hometown, Kamie thought she and I must have run across each other at some point. Little did I know, my next victim was just around the corner, or, literally, three miles from my parents' house. It's funny how people can live so close to each other without a clue of the other's existence until the right time. Halie's parents knew my grandmother. We grew up in the same small town and had some mutual friends. She had even succeeded in driving *around* the Kodak photo hut instead of *through* it. Halie and I were avid animal watchers, of both the four-legged and two-legged species and enjoyed doing many of the same activities. However, our meeting was not meant to be until the day Mom was at her wit's end trying to find someone to be my personal assistant and contacted Kamie to see if she possibly had any leads on full or part-time help. I had placed her name in my rolodex in case I wanted to hit her up for a job, but never imagined it would be Kamie who led us to my next assistant so quickly. Arrangements to meet were made so the details of the job could be discussed. Halie happened to come along for the ride that day. And what a ride it turned out to be! After mulling over the idea of a career change for some time, she decided to join me and become my full-time personal assistant.

Halie was a single mother raising a son, working two to three jobs on average. Her opaque blue eyes and strong Indian face showed signs of undue stress and sadness that had been collecting through the years. The Center was going through an operational change and becoming a state facility instead of continuing under the control of its local board members. All of these transitions translated into more responsibility, more paperwork, and more headaches at essentially the same salary for Halie. Sharing the same warped sense of humor helped in bonding us together, but for many reasons, Halie's decision to leave her stressful job to be my assistant came easily. It's funny how wrong first impressions can be. When Halie told us she was interested in taking the job, my first thought was, why in the world would anyone leave a good job with benefits to work for me with no benefits and no opportunities to move up the career ladder. Her five-foot eight-inch frame looked strong, healthy and vibrant. However, the more I got to know her, the more I realized she was the opposite of Zoey. Even though she was strong on the outside, her core was crumbling from a lifetime of disappointments and defeat. Both of her parents had died from heart trouble. She suffered from the same fate as many women—attracting the wrong type of men. Her heart and soul were terribly bruised and broken. However, unlike Zoey's and my disability, Halie could mask her weaknesses.

Not long before Halie started working with me, her

mother, who was the last major support in her life, suddenly passed away. Because her beloved mother's death was so unexpected, Halie was battling unresolved issues that churned and twisted until a tornado formed within her soul. Years of feeling like no one truly loved her, except her father who had passed on when Halie was only a teenager, left her desolate and vulnerable. Though she was a few years older than me, her inner child had never stopped crying out, "this is not the way I am supposed to be loved."

The cliché, misery loves company, could not have fit us better. Everyone knows a drowning person cannot save another drowning person. Someone must know how to swim. In my finite mind, I truly thought that since Halie and I were both battling our own personal tornados we could someday conquer them together and come out on top. Relationships rarely work out as they do in algebra. Though two negative numbers become positive in math, two negative people rarely come out positively unscathed. We gave helping one another out of depression and negativity our best shot. We did each other more harm than good. The fact that I had a counseling degree but could not help Halie with her depression made me feel increasingly useless. The terrorizing thought that "this is not the way it's supposed to be" became my consuming perception of reality. When our tornados co-mingled, the suction pulling us downward was exponentially multiplied and sometimes made normal functioning impossible. However, on the good days when we ventured out of our holes, we were like jack-in-the boxes sprung into surprise and wonder.

Old friends have told me I met my match when Halie came along. That was a good thing. Other times, it was downright scary. I delight in playing a good "gotcha!" on deserving and unsuspecting persons. There is nothing more enjoyable than witnessing one backfire right before my very eyes. In the years I worked with Halie, there were several attempts to outdo each other's "gotchas!" but few were as memorable as the one at the Texas Capitol.

Texas has an annual "Disability Day at the Capitol." On this day, people with disabilities are encouraged to come and rally in front of the State Capitol for breakfast, lunch and a chance to meet with local representatives. One of the advocacy groups I had contacted invited me to go along with them and participate in the day's activities. I must say, it was an awesome experience to witness so many people converge together on the Capitol grounds for the same cause.

As the festivities came to a close, Halie and I decided to go to the gift shop to see if there were any souvenirs that screamed, *buy me.* I found some things and went to the register to pay. I did not see Halie, so I went out the door to look for her. Out of the corner of my eye, I saw her talking to a nice-looking, middle-aged security guard while pointing in my direction. That concerned me a bit, but I shrugged it off and presumed that Hallie was flirting as she often enjoyed doing. But then they started walking towards me, each with a serious look on their face. As they came closer, I overheard her tell the guard, "Officer, I saw this woman shoplifting in the gift shop and I think you should strip-search her."

I could not believe what she was saying! I've been known to do some crazy things, *however* I'm not insane! I would never commit such a crime, especially in the State Capitol. Not knowing what the heck to say or do, I looked wide-eyed at the guard and nervously burst into laughter. Thank goodness he was no fool and had a sense of humor. He took one good look at me, turned to Halie and sarcastically said, "Yeah right, what did you put under her seat?"

This particular leadership group led me to many wonderful people as I became more involved in advocacy. Even though I didn't completely agree with many of their tactics, I'd be hard-pressed to find a better group of people. In the business world, it's a well-known fact that you have to give something to get something. However, many well-meaning advocacy and policy-changing groups adhere to the military philosophy of, "kill and take no hostages." Seminars are strategically held throughout the year, to inform advocates of cutting-edge legislative news, and to refuel the sparks that may have been blown out from the daily grind of helping others. Sometimes there was an opportunity to meet someone that might just "leave footprints" on your heart and change you forever in the best way possible. For me, that person was Joseph.

I wish I could tell you our eyes met across a crowded room

and it was love at first sight but that is reserved for fairy tales and I live in the real world. A pair of eyes did indeed meet mine from across a crowded hotel lobby, but it was not Joseph's. It was his dog's. The dog trick always works on me! Joseph's tall, lean frame rose from the reservation desk and his deep, ebony eyes followed the path of his faithful dog and rested squarely on mine. We went to dinner the next night. Dinner led to higher phone bills and unforgettable excursions. Jo was much more ambulatory than I was and could drive. This was very useful, and he wore out a set of tires driving back and forth from Austin, which allowed us to often gaze into each other's eyes. Over dinner we discovered that along with sharing many similar childhood experiences growing up with cerebral palsy, we both have a Bachelor in Business and a Masters in Rehabilitation Counseling. And, we were often accused by friends and family of having "unusual" senses of humor and insatiable appetites for adventure. It's sad though, what miserable people do to try and fill the emptiness inside.

During this brief yet wonderfully exciting time with Jo, I unfortunately misused sex as I had misused the Vacuum Club. It was an escape from my reality, which is what I longed for. Knowing Jo desired me more than leveled life's playing field. He made me feel beautiful, which is what every woman wants to feel. I felt "normal" when we were together. I thought, *this* is how life is "supposed to be." To quote the classic Aretha Franklin song, "I felt like a natural woman."

When I was safe in his arms, I was anesthetized to the pain and anger in my world and entered another world in which my senses were revitalized.

Unfortunately, the wonderful feeling didn't last long and it certainly was not meant to be shared by two unmarried people, no matter how committed they felt towards one another. There is no doubt that Joseph and I loved each other. However, it did not take long for us to realize that I was too engrossed in what I thought were the injustices of my life and eventually, my anger drove him far away. Though we might have gone where angels fear to tread while we were together, I know a few must have been watching over us during some of our antics.

On a long weekend late in the summer, Halie, her childhood friend Kim, and I decided to take a fast and furious trip to Austin where Jo lived. While there, Joseph gave me one of the most romantic evenings of my life. It started with dinner at my favorite Italian restaurant. I truly believe God ordained Italian food to be served in heaven. We even sing about it in church. That is what the line is referring to in the hymn, *This Is My Story*. "Oh, what a foretaste of glory divine." Frankly, I can hardly wait to see what's on the all-you-can-eat pasta buffet for only $0.00!

After a wonderful dinner complete with a heavenly piece of chocolate cake and coffee, we strolled down Sixth Street. Those who are familiar with the Austin area know Sixth Street is the place to be on a Thursday night. I despise the act of staring at people but looking at some of the sights we beheld merited two or three quick glances back. I had always considered myself a pretty worldly person, but it appeared as if I had indeed entered "a brave new world!" There were people who had rings and things coming from every orifice of their body. Not only was it "in" to be scantily clad, it seemed necessary in order to show off body art.

After browsing in some of the stores, a beautiful horse drawn carriage caught my eye. I had always wanted to ride away in one and live happily ever after, so we did the next best thing. Halie and Kim found a way to hoist me into the carriage and gave Joseph a helping hand up. It was kind of a "push me, pull you" type of project but we all made it in one piece. At that point, instead of trying to discreetly gawk at the "coming attractions" walking by, the shoe was on the other foot. *We* were the sight to behold now. The driver asked where we wanted to go as he whisked us away through the crowded street. We didn't have a destination in mind, so we giddily answered that we would go wherever he would take us. The poor driver looked as if he thought it might be a long night when we loaded into the carriage, but now he knew it was a sure thing. From the list of choices he gave us, we chose to go around the Capitol and a nearby park in the same vicinity. Not only did the driver have to put up with our silliness, he also had to fight off "hitchhikers" who were jumping onto the running boards trying to catch a free ride.

Taking advantage of the situation, I snuggled up to

Joseph as he put his arm around me and once again, I felt totally safe. The full moon was absolutely breathtaking as it reflected off of the statues on the Capitol grounds. Lights behind the stained-glass windows of the building gave it a majestic aura as the horse trotted us around the premises. Stars were shining brilliantly in the night sky even though the city was lit up as brightly as the noonday sun. I wished time could stand still for a while. Wanting to savor the last few moments of the ride, a hush fell over us as we neared our point of return. The sound of horse's hooves trotting on the pavement along with the moon was hypnotic. As we journeyed along, the driver loosened up and began making polite conversation with Halie. People tend to say the funniest things when they are trying to compliment a person with disabilities. They mean well, but what comes out of their mouths does not always sound polite. The driver was telling Halie that it took a special kind of person to do the type of work she did and praised her "for being so good to them."

Joseph turned it around and said, "Well, *somebody* has to be nice to them."

Chapter 8
1998-2002

Out of my tornado, and into the marvelous light.

I was devastated when Joseph left, even though he and I both knew it was best for his own well-being. He was a gentle soul, and my hostility was chipping away at him. Realizing and accepting this truly broke my heart. Not only did I feel like a total failure at getting a job and at helping Halie out of a major depression, (which I was trained in school to help people overcome), but my sense of failure also encompassed feeling incompetent as a daughter. I was still sponging off my parents at the age of thirty-five, with no hopes of employment in sight. Both Mom and Dad had always been very goal-oriented, however, I had quit setting goals for myself. My reasoning was—if I did not strive to meet any goals, I would avoid feeling even more disgusted and disappointed with myself if I didn't reach them. And, as if this train of thought was not defeating enough, now I felt like a colossal failure at holding on to the man who, I thought, I was supposed to spend the rest of my life with. The tornado in me was picking up speed with each passing day. Sara McLachlan's song "Angel" hit the top of the charts around that time and quickly became my personal anthem. I sang it at least ten times a day. I related to it so much at that point, I asked Halie to have it played at my funeral.

"Spend all your time waiting for that second chance
for a break that would make it okay there's always one reason
to feel not good enough
and it's hard at the end of the day I need some distraction
oh beautiful release
memory seeps from my veins let me be empty
and weightless and maybe I'll find some peace tonight in the
arms of an angel
fly away from here
from this dark cold hotel room and the endlessness that you fear
you are pulled from the wreckage of your silent reverie
you're in the arms of the angel may you find some comfort there
so tired of the straight line
and everywhere you turn
there's vultures and thieves at your back and the storm keeps on
twisting
you keep on building the lie it don't make no difference escaping
one last time
it's easier to believe in this sweet madness oh
this glorious sadness that brings me to my knees."

I was in a morbid state of mind. Certainly not to be confused with "a New York state of mind." I had stopped making goals in order to numb the fear of failing again, and I had no one to call my own. I survived like a feather blowing in a gusting wind. The only time I stuck my head out was when we traveled. My poor father continued to finance my escapades in hopes of incentivizing me to reconnect with the real activities of daily living, such as getting dressed and going to work. During this topsy-turvy time, Amanda and Bailey did their best to lift my spirits, while also helping me get my feet back on the ground. It just so happened that I was on one of my treks to see them when we heard the tail end of a radio ad for the Fleetwood Mac Reunion Tour concert. Unfortunately, neither Halie nor I caught when or where it was, so I placed it on the back burner of my mind for later research. One good thing that I could always count on was Halie and Bailey's willingness to meet half-way to pick me up or drop me off. They always had such a loving way of making me feel special. Referring to the meeting point as the pick up or drop off made it sound as if I was dealing an illegal substance. Secretly, I think Bailey enjoyed the drop off, much more than the pickup. (I still keep trying to convince him that having me around is truly a joy in disguise. He continues to assure me that the "joy" he feels when I'm with him is well-disguised.)

This time, when returning home from Bailey and Manda's, the meeting point was Dallas around 2 p.m. If all went as planned, everyone could be back in their own homes by dark. As usual, Halie surprised me by announcing that we were staying overnight in Dallas. She had brought her friend and faithful sidekick, Kim, along to help with the drive back. They had already decided before they picked me up that it would be fun to eat at Planet Hollywood. I did my best to be a stick-in-the-mud and convince them that I was much too exhausted to go. The previous "midnight madness" sessions with Amanda had caught up with me big time. Halie and Kim won the tug-of-war of wills. Thank goodness they did, because I got so much more that night than a blue plate special.

It is a no-brainer that I've been a big fan of Stevie Nick's music for a long time. (Her name being mentioned in the first chapter wasn't a coincidence.) No, I am not the mad stalker on wheels. I just have had a great admiration for her abilities ever since she started with the group, Fleetwood Mac. When we heard they were going to do their last reunion tour, Halie and I talked about going but never made any definitive plans. I was ready and willing to go see Fleetwood Mac perform anywhere we could get tickets. Halie was not as excited as I was about going to see a classic rock band. So, I planned to bide my time and waited impatiently for them to do what they came to do.

Among the many skills I've managed to fine-tune is my ability to eavesdrop, especially when the information is juicy. It's been said that bolts of lights radiate from my head and I look like the character, Beetlejuice. Some call it a curse, but I can't help it if folks have no sense of humor as it relates to my gift. Whether good or bad, my "gift" yielded high returns that night. Halie and Kim were engrossed in a discussion about the decor of the restaurant while I was in my own world, enjoying my hamburger. My ears perked up like my dog's ears when I thought I heard Fleetwood Mac mentioned at the table parallel to ours. I tried to nonchalantly do a giraffe move and periscope my neck over to their table. At times like this, it would be advantageous to have extendable body parts like Jim Carey's character in *The Mask*. Halie noticed the veins popping out on my neck and asked what in the world I was doing.

"Sssshhhh," I said. "I thought I heard something about Fleetwood Mac over at that table! Ask the waiter when he passes by to ask them what they were talking about."

Luckily, the waiter was not bashful and did just that. The couple was kind enough to inform us that the concert started in an hour at the fairgrounds. Not knowing exactly where we were going, Halie and I looked at each other and simultaneously said, "There is no way we can make it in an hour and still buy tickets in time. Let's go!!!"

So off we went on another adventure. We knew we were near the vicinity of the fairgrounds when we saw taillights lined up for miles. When we left Planet Hollywood, money was the last thing on our minds. That quickly changed when we arrived at the entrance gate and the parking attendant asked us for $7.50. The infamous, dumbfounded, deer-in-headlights look came over each of our faces. Halie reached into her purse and luckily found the right amount of change to get in. Then, she frantically ordered us to look in our purses, change-holder, and the floorboard of the van to see how much money we could pool together. We were Periscoping for Pennies instead of *Dialing for Dollars.* Before moving on any further, Halie asked the parking lot attendant what the chances were of getting three tickets. She smiled and said the words we were all dreading.

"Forget that! This baby has been sold out for a while now. But you can't turn around here. You'll have to follow this road all the way to the opposite side to get to the exit gate."

It was as if the air had been sucked out of the van. We could already hear musicians warming up on stage, so we knew the odds of finding tickets for a "reasonable" price was practically zero. We tried to turn around to make our way to the exit but couldn't, because of the two other lanes of traffic that were blocking us in. We continued to inch slowly to the front and onward towards the exit on the opposite side.

Some call it a lucky coincidence. Others, destiny. Whatever it was, you've probably never seen three people more excited to see a man selling tickets in front of the amphitheater as we were. Yes, the usual name for people who do that sort of thing is "scalpers," but believe me, it would not apply to him that night by any stretch of the imagination. Luckily, at that point, we were in the inside lane and could drive into the loading zone beside him without totally stopping traffic.

"Got three tickets with your name on them for $275.00," he said.

We all gasped. We were not sure if we had $7.50, let alone $275.00! Halie laughed and said no, but thanks. The man quickly countered with $230.00. Halie, being *the* nit-wit she was said, "No, but if my friend here gets out on the corner, I'm sure she can raise that kind of money in no time."

Thank goodness the man had a sense of humor and chuckled because I certainly did not. He then said, "Okay $195.00."

I was beginning to feel as if we were doing the "how low can you go" limbo! By that time, what looked to be a fifty-foot, chocolate brown limousine pulled up in front of us to unload passengers. Parking there felt claustrophobic because there were cars lined up on each side of us. We were jam packed in there. People were rushing by us towards the main entrance. Chances of getting in were looking very slim again. I think the man was close to exasperation because he realized the concert was starting and he had spent the last twenty minutes with three women who apparently did not have the funds that he had hoped to make from those tickets.

He finally propped his elbow in the window with his head in hand and said "Okay, okay, how much can you pay me?" By then we had searched in every crevice of our purses, and the van and had come up with $139.47. Halie gingerly handed him the $139 in bills and the .47 in dimes, nickels and pennies.

As he was counting it, he muttered, "You do know this is even below the price that I paid. Who's scalping whom? This ain't supposed to happen."

I started to sing, "welcome to my world. Won't you come on in!" I guess he was just glad to finally be rid of the tickets, and us because he sighed, rolled his eyes, took the money and ran!

In the meantime, we had caught the eye of the guy directing traffic. He noticed the disabled license plate on my van and was wildly waving his arms for us to park in a parking space he had reserved for us. This was quite a feat because he had to block three lanes of traffic and hold the parking space open while we maneuvered the van over to where he was standing. Remember the limo that had pulled up just inches in front of us? Well, we got to see it up close and personal. As we were pulling out, making a hard left, we felt a slight nudge. I thought we had just run over some minor object in the road, so I yelled at Halie to continue crossing over towards the space. Nonetheless, the young limo driver took our actions to be anything but minor and bolted out of his car like a roman candle, wildly waving his arms at us, screaming, "Stop, stop! You hit my car!"

So now we had *two* men waving wildly at us and three lanes of blocked traffic waiting on us to do something. One of them was yelling for us to go while the other was crazily grabbing onto the hood of the van screaming for us to stop. Having two cute guys wildly waving and grabbing for us could have indeed been an excerpt from a good dream. However, in the present situation, it was a down right nightmare. Halie did not know what to do except park to get out of the flow of mainstream traffic. When she didn't stop, the limo driver yelled, "Hey, hey, what's your name? Do you have insurance?" The other guy holding the parking space for us caught on to what was happening and started yelling at him to let us park. The tenacious driver finally saw that the empty parking space was only about twenty feet away from where we were and backed off so that we could get out of the bottleneck we had created. However, his hand never left the side of our van as we crossed over into the parking space. He was hot on our trail!

By the time we finally parked, forty minutes had passed. There's nothing like a memorable entrance. By this time, the commotion of all the yelling and flailing of hands had also attracted the attention of a policeman. Usually Halie would have enjoyed having several men awaiting her arrival, but not this time. All eyes were waiting for her to emerge from the van. Not really knowing what to expect, Halie cautiously got out of the car like a suspected criminal. (Her reputation for being a hardened criminal preceded our arrival!) I don't know what they were thinking but they all swarmed around her and bombarded her with questions as she walked around the van to get me out. One of the brightest of the three men looked at Halie and said, "Hey, hey, you're not even disabled." She tried to keep from laughing for fear it would make matters worse, said "wait a minute," and pushed the lever on the back of my van to open the door and let down my ramp. Now she really captured their attention. For all they knew, she could have been unloading a vehicle full of terrorists or aliens. By the looks on their faces, I couldn't tell whether they were relieved or disappointed when I slowly rolled out and gently smiled.

After the hoopla, all the men said was, "Oh, you are disabled!" and walked away. Oh, and as for the "dent" in the limo, it turned out to be a tiny scratch that buffed out as we stood there. The driver became very quiet when Halie whipped out the camera and documented the evidence.

Another outstanding trip in Halie's and my crazy voyages was when we took her son Tony on a little jaunt down memory lane for spring break his freshman year in college. During our four plus years together, Halie and I tried to take Tony somewhere exciting for each of his spring breaks. This time, Halie decided we should visit some of their dear friends on a ranch in Arizona where Halie had been the caretaker while Tony was in preschool. Trying to be the best single mom she could be, Halie always tried to work jobs that allowed her to spend a lot of quality time with Tony as he grew up. They told me so many tales of their days of adventurous hikes in Arizona through dry riverbeds to an unbelievably beautiful turquoise waterfall where they had many picnics. I wanted to see it for myself. This one was destined from the start to go down in our history book.

Halie had spent days trying to organize and pack our

clothes for eight fun-filled days, and it showed. We took out the middle seat of my tan Chevy van to make more room for the menagerie of luggage, plus two large dogs. Halie was feeling so good about finding space for everything until Tony, her charming, wise-cracking offspring, came home from school. He opened the van door to load his stuff, took one look and said, "Mom what have you been smoking? So glad to be driving to Arizona looking like the Beverly Hillbillies while all my friends are spending their spring break partying at Cozumel or Padre Island." I caught the glint in his puppy dog brown eyes that screamed, *let's put Jonean on the van roof.* I would be an outstanding cheap imitation of "Granny" in her rocking chair, and he could have room to stretch out his five foot eight, iron pumped, seventeen-year old physique. You see, Halie had done such a great packing job that she forgot to leave enough room for her own beloved baby boy!

After a very long day on the road, every creature in our van was asking when we would get there. Though our two Boxers loved to go for rides and feel the wind flapping their ears and jowls, they were even vocalizing, *enough is enough.* Halie told me the ranch was on a dirt road a few miles off the main highway. It was naive of me to presume that she meant maybe three to six miles from the road. The nice, double-wide, desert paradise home was more than twelve plus miles off an unbeaten path that looked as if only the early pioneers or UFO's could travel on them. Speaking of aliens, it's amazing how much those tall, sequoia cacti favor willowy creatures from the unknown. Call it paranoia, call it a guilty conscience, but by the time we reached the eight-mile marker, I began to wonder if Halie had an ulterior motive for bringing me to such a desolate place. Aside from the gorgeous desert scenery, I really didn't know what to expect. Both Tony and Halie had jokingly told me the facilities provided an "out" without the "house" behind the bush on the side of the double wide. Thank goodness they upgraded to indoor plumbing since Halie had left. I would have really been down and out if I had needed to use the out. My mind went through the list of possibilities she might have been paying me back for. Heaven knows, she had plenty to choose from. It looked like the ideal place to "knock" someone off just as she had knocked off the van's license plate going around a scary curve and into the very large pothole. It would take days or maybe months to find a body out there. However, I finally concluded that if indeed Halie planned on killing me, she would not do it in front of our three children.

Then, my stirring thoughts turned towards the family we were staying with. All I really knew about them was that they were deeply religious people who ran a first-class nursing home at one time and helped Halie with Tony during his formative years. What if their religion had a new commandment and now they believed in sacrificing middle-aged disabled women? My mind snapped back to reality. From all that I had ever read, in order to be a good sacrifice, one had to be pure. I was safe. As it turned out, they were a gracious, tightly knit family. Each of them had a rich personality yet maintained a very strong bond that was inspiring to see. They reminded me of a happy, semi-functional family in a Tennessee Williams play.

Kate, the lady of the ranch, had a fiery but humorous personality, and ruled the whole ramrod with a velvet fist. Her unforgettably boisterous nature put me in the mind of a modern-day Scarlett O'Hara. Kate's fading blond hair, kept neatly pinned up, gave her a commanding look that suited her tall, robust body. Even though she happened to be the middle child of five, when Kate spoke, everyone jumped, not out of fear, but out of respect. She had a way of making people feel important so everyone wanted to do more to please her.

It was not unusual for Kate and her husband Robert to invite anywhere from five to forty-five guests over for Sabbath dinner, and then have the same number of people in the kitchen either preparing or cleaning up afterwards. Robert was a very intense, service-built man who enjoyed having deep, philosophical debates with anyone willing to challenge his wits. His large eagle tattoo matched his caring yet independent truck driver spirit. He was remarkably learned on a variety of subjects, considering his formal education was limited to around the eighth grade level. Robert was proof that the school of hard knocks and a good heart could sometimes get one further than having a degree. This could be seen clearly not only in the possessions he had accumulated through hard work, but also by the people who loved to be around him. Robert and Kate both possess riches that extend way beyond wealth.

Kate's sister, Iris was an equally fascinating character, and I do mean character. Her salt and pepper, straight hair complemented her lean and lanky body. She reminded me of a woman from the last frontier. There was no task too great or too small that Iris could not accomplish on that ranch if she set her mind to it. When she discovered my love for horses and adventure, it wasn't long until she, Halie, and Kate figured a way to get me onto her horse, Chester, so I could make the trek to the enchanting waterfall. It was quite a ways, so we decided it would be best if I rode most of the way on a three wheeler with Halie, and then climbed atop Chester to ride up the steep, rocky pathway to the waterfall.

Mounting me on Chester resembled a redneck volleyball game gone awry. A gleam in Halie's eye told me I was undoubtedly the ball. Two people were on the left side of the horse trying to find the best place to grab on to in order to hoist me on, while four more hands in the air on the right side waited to push me back over in case I went too far and missed the saddle. Iris, the referee, held Chester's head and reigns to ensure the "net" didn't move.

My ride on Chester was much smoother than the teeth-jarring buggy ride. I swore Halie was trying to drive me to my grave on the three-wheeler, going over every bump she could find in the dry riverbed leading to the waterfall. The whole experience was a blast.

There isn't anything sweeter in life than pulling a good prank on a deserving friend. It was especially rewarding when I could pull an embarrassing "gotcha" on Halie, because, as you have seen, she pulled one on me every time an opportunity arose. As stated previously, it was not unusual for Kate and Robert to have people coming out of the woodworks on weekends. I was truly enjoying meeting people and getting to know everyone's personality. Everything was running smoothly until I tried to be "smooth" in front of an old friend of the family's. Halie had mentioned that Jeff, one of Kate's nephews whom she had taken in to raise when he was younger, was cute, but cute did not do him justice. His deep-set dark, green eyes, short, dark brown hair and well-built body immediately caught my eye. As usual, the more attractive I think a guy is, the dumber the questions I ask. Thank goodness Tony saved the conversation before I got too many stretch marks from trying to fit my foot in my mouth.

Since Jeff was taking a production class and in the midst of making a movie for a class project, he and Tony became engrossed in conversation about the movies they wanted to make someday. They both had good ideas for story lines and special effects that were sure to make "box office hits." Halie and I were amazed at the details they had already worked out in their minds. I asked Jeff if he had thought of the actors he would like to fill the major roles in his future movies. He surprisingly answered very seriously. We, of course suggested, that he could give Tony his big break in show biz by casting him in a leading role. Then I added "And to really help the rest of us, if you ever have a role that calls for a woman with a disability, I know where you can find a very qualified person to fill it." Sensing they all thought they knew where this was headed, I did a 180 and said, "Please feel free to call Halie. She will be more than glad to help you out." For once, she was speechless.

After about four and a half years of living with Halie, those "gotchas" ceased being funny and turned spiteful. I think both of us had unconsciously built up a high wall of resentment and became set on not improving each other's lot in life any more than we already had. I truly resented her for not helping me more in the job-hunting department when in her former job, she had been able to place other people with disabilities. However, looking back now, if Halie had helped me find a job, I undoubtedly would have missed out on some of life's abundance, and this book might not have had as many crazy tales as it does. Our tornadoes intermingled for so long, and the debris was strewn so high and wide, we were suffocating from the destruction. We both knew the day would come when Halie would have to leave, but neither of us planned it to be so soon. Halie had quit several times before; however, I always talked her into staying and riding out the storm, but the last time she quit, I did nothing to block the door and regretfully told her it was probably for the best.

Sometimes you need to endure the pain of a break before you can become whole. The day Halie drove away, my spirit finally slipped through the eye of my tornado and I was crushed. However, Christ beautifully caught the shattered, jagged pieces that swirled destructively through the air and amazingly began to rebuild me with the strength to quiet my tornado, instead of allowing it to rage destructively within me. I want to leave you with a chuckle in your heart and a smile on your face as you read the last page of this chapter, so on that note, I've decided to include the down and dirty tale of Halie's and my last escapade. Old friends have repeatedly told me that if I wrote down every quirky situation I've found myself in, people would claim I was either taking some powerful hallucinogens or was a first-class liar. The adage that life is stranger than fiction is true, especially as it relates to my life. Contrary to how you may have pictured me from the stories in this book, I am shy around people I do not know, and in crowds. One of my deepest desires growing up was to be inconspicuous. However, sitting in a big, bulky wheelchair tends to have the opposite effect. Even the best designer camouflage could not hide the matching braces on both my teeth and legs, not to mention the shiny chrome on the wheelchair. Dressing up as the Tin Man in the Wizard of Oz was always a "shoe-in" for me on Halloween. As you also know, Halloween has proven to be a dangerously bewitching time for me.

The last Halloween Halie and I were together, we took advantage of the inexpensive specials many airlines were offering during that period and flew up North. Halie had always bragged about the beautiful fall colors that Idaho was famous for and had been asking me to go there with her for years. It seemed to be a good time to go. So, off we went on another adventure. At that time, security was tightening up airport procedures all across the country because of 9/11. The sight of guards with machine guns at different checkpoints in the halls was not what we were accustomed to seeing and, quite frankly, a bit intimidating. Halie can attest to this. She was sent all the way back to the baggage check-in counter for carrying a small pair of needle nosed scissors in her backpack. When it was her turn to walk through the metal detector, the alarms went off. Watching all eyes turn our way was humorous, but also embarrassing. Halie, with her warped sense of humor decided it was not enough for all the attention to be on her. Oh no! She wanted to share the spotlight by dragging me into the tense situation. It goes without saying that with all the metal surrounding me on my wheelchair, lights, bells, and whistles go off when I am within a five-foot radius of any metal detector. And, no, it's not because of a metal plate in my head, as many friends claim it to be.

When the security guards saw me coming through the entrance and started yelling, "Female needed for pat down," I was suddenly thrust back into the sixth grade, looking for a big desk to crawl under. In spite of turning a shade of pink, we proceeded onward to a woman guard. Do not ask me why, but people who are in this line of work rarely seem to have a good sense of humor. This was especially true after September

11th proved that we were not as secure as we once thought we were. The woman smiled and gently started a hand check on me to make sure I was not as armed and dangerous as I looked.

Seizing the moment, Halie said, "Excuse me, but don't you know that she prefers a male to do that?"

Not really knowing how to respond, the guard and I both chuckled, hoping the awkward moment would pass quickly.

It didn't. Halie added, "Oh yes, the only way I can get her to fly is by telling her a cute, male guard will do the pat down."

That big desk I was wishing for didn't feel adequate to hide the embarrassment turning my entire body the shade of crimson. I was speechless, so I laughed hysterically and inwardly threatened vindication sooner, rather than later. If I wasn't afraid that we wouldn't have been kept there another hour, I would have claimed she'd been smoking crack again. To move the uncomfortable situation along, everyone laughed and did their part to hurriedly send us on our way. It was quite silly of me to think she would drop this madness once we were past the first security checkpoint. When Halie was on a roll, she was relentless. She told every armed guard we passed that she thought I looked suspicious and it would greatly ease her mind if they would search me. By that point, it was a good thing I was not armed because she was dangerously close to getting on my bad side.

Relief washed over me when we finally reached the pre-boarding area. For some reason I thought she would drop the shenanigans as we prepared to load the plane. But I underestimated her tenacious, relentless spirit. A twinkle appeared in her eye as she saw the nice man coming to help me onto the plane and I could only imagine what was headed out of her mouth. I needed to think fast in order to stop this madness. Sure enough, Halie did not disappoint.

"Excuse me," she said, "I think you should check her one more time. Something about her looks suspicious."

Thank goodness, the guy just laughed and reached down to unlock my break to roll me down the landing. About the time he touched my chair, I said, "Excuse me, I don't think you know me that well. But I'm sure that lady wouldn't mind if you patted her down. She likes that sort of thing, you know." That shut her up for a while.

The trip was a "real trip" because it ended just as crazily as it began. We spent four, fun-filled days toodling around the countryside in a '69 Chevy Impala with Jade, another one of Halie's childhood best friends. The car was as classic as its owner. The dark, golden, metallic Chevy looked like a combination of Austin Power's and Uncle Buck's cars. The interior was a fashionable yellow and lime green shag carpet with the original leather seats. Jade said when anything wore out on that car, there was nothing that couldn't be fixed with a little wire and duct tape. Just like most of the people in Halie's life, Jade was a character. She reminded me of a modern-day Janis Joplin. Her dark eyes and semi-stringy, straight hair reflected that era. She was an independent, five-foot four inch, free spirited flower child straight out of the 1960's who would give you the shirt off her back if she thought you needed it. In fact, that had probably been her biggest fault in life. People saw her good heart and took advantage of it so often it left her like some candles, burnt on both ends, soft in the very center, with a hard outer shell.

One of the highlights of the trip was touring the local cheese factory. It was well worth the ride in the back-seat of the strange smelling car Halie and I had rented. It smelled as if someone or *something* had met their maker in the trunk. The aroma of all that fresh cheese was quite exhilarating after the smelly ride. Even the worst smelling cheese had a refreshing odor compared to the reeking smell of our car. I begged Halie to just leave me in the sample section instead of making me fold up in half to fit back in that smelly tin can on wheels. I promised to be as quiet as a mouse in a cheese factory. To that remark, Halie replied, "I always knew you were a rat."

One of the big weekly events in Jade's hood was Karaoke night at Sam's. Karaoke night was similar to a comedy club on amateur night. No matter how bad the participants were, the longer they were on stage, the better they thought they became. It was one of the "wonders" of the world. No offense to anyone who was brave enough to show off their hidden talents, but some of them left you thinking that they should just bury their musical talent altogether. True to form, I was tickled when Jade and Halie got up to sing. Simultaneously, I also got the urge to sing a different song. You've heard it before: "Gotta go, gotta go, gotta go." The urge hit me with a mighty force. Don't misunderstand me. They did a great job singing. Halie always did a good job on Patsy Cline's songs. It's just that when they were staring intently at the monitor, trying to read the lyrics, they looked like two scared chickens in a KFC line up about to become the "full meal deal" of the day! My laughter soon turned into serious business and I practically screamed at poor Halie that I had to be excused, now!

Thank goodness, there was a big bathroom with no stalls to maneuver into. It is doubtful I could have made it without an easy entrance. However, by the time everything was set to go, I could not go. No amount of warm or cold running water helped. Halie thought maybe a little privacy might help. The door was not even five feet away from our table and could clearly be seen. Oh, what a relief to discover that privacy did do the trick. However, I got an extra adventure because of it. The door opened and a face appeared, but it was not Halie's. The nice woman said, "Oh, excuse me, dear. Here, let me lock the door for you," and quickly closed it behind her.

About the time the door started closing, Halie realized what was happening and was on her feet making a dash for the door. Jade said it looked like a slow-motion movie with the actress bounding across a crowded room, screaming "Noooooooooooooooooo!" in a low muffled voice. The damage had been done by the time Halie reached the door. I actually felt sorry for the woman when I heard Halie say in her not so diplomatic voice, "Please don't tell me you locked that door."

The woman replied, "Why yes, I thought she could use some privacy."

I could feel the temperature in the tiny bathroom rise as Halie explained that it was impossible for me to get into my manual chair because the brakes were lousy brakes and that was why she left it unlocked in the first place. The poor woman left after that.

So there I was, a sitting duck in yet another bathroom. I couldn't help but wonder if God was trying to get my attention, or if it was just a funny coincidence. I didn't have much time to entertain these wonderfully deep thoughts before I heard the dreaded words, "Let's just break the door down!"

I panicked and thought, "Oh, please don't, I do not want that kind of exposure."

Halie yelled, "Don't worry, the manager has gone to find the key. Unfortunately, after twenty minutes of searching, no keys were to be found on the premises, so a pipe-wrench turned out to be the next best thing."

Not wanting to be "caught with my pants down," I managed to pull them up right before the door flew open. What can you say in an awkward situation like this, with four pairs of eyeballs staring intently at you? The only thing that came to my mind was. "Excuse me, do you really think you know me this well!"

Epilogue

Not long ago, a friend asked me if I really thought a disability is joy in disguise. In other words, do I really walk the walk, or more appropriately, ride the ride? To answer this question honestly, I would have to say no. A disability is not always a joy. It should come as no surprise that it would be slightly difficult to call the times when I was stuck, a true joy. Not wishing for the ability to walk out of those predicaments would be abnormal or even a bit creepy. Let's face it, there's only so much graffiti that can distract a person from the fact that they're trapped in a bathroom at the mercy of people on the other side of the door.

I believe living with a disability can be similar to having some of the best times of your life that you don't recognize as such until it's all over because of the frustration you faced in the moment. Nonetheless, after it's all said and done, I often say, wow, wasn't that a ride! From the snapshots of my life in this book, you can see that because of my disability, I've been allowed to share my life on a more intimate level with a variety of people, of whom I likely never would have otherwise. Granted, I would have gladly passed on some of the "eye-opening experiences" that have come my way. However, I would not have wanted to miss out on the abundance of life's adventures—good or bad. God used the presence of each of these special individuals to help me color outside of the lines of my expectations. Some of these experiences, disguised as simple, every day, mundane tasks, have become some of the greatest joys in my memory. It could've been because of a goofy look or an unexpected giggle. Isn't finding joy in the simple things part of the meaning and blessing of abundant life?

In John 10:10, Jesus says He did not come as "the thief who comes only to steal and kill and destroy, He came that they may have life, and have it more abundantly." This is one of those wonderful verses in the Bible that holds multiple treasures for us to discover. Of course, at first glance we can gather that Jesus is talking about eternal life. He came into this world and died for our sins so when we physically die, it is far from "the end" for us. We still have an abundantly, perfect life to live with Him in heaven. However, that is just the icing on the end piece of a double frosted cake! I think Jesus had abundantly more in mind when He spoke those words. The more days God graciously gives me to experience life on this planet, the more I'm convinced that the abundant life on earth includes the bad times along with the good ones. How else can the Apostle Paul have made this claim in Philippians 4:11-13: *I am not saying this because I am in need, for I have learned to be content whatever the circumstances. I know what it is to be in need, and I know what it is to have plenty. I have learned the secret of being content in any and every situation, whether well fed or hungry, whether living in plenty or in want. I can do everything through him who gives me strength.*

From this verse, I gather that Paul's life was no steady picnic. He knew what it was like to live at the extremes of existence. I imagine in the midst of everything going on around him, Paul undoubtedly experienced some of the same "tornado" feelings I've felt, where he wanted to scream, "this is not the way it's supposed to be, *especially* after he completely surrendered his life to the Lord. This thought may have crossed his mind a few times while he was locked up in chains. Paul was probably tempted to bargain with God and say, "Okay God, you know, I am totally down with your will and have stopped killing your people. Wherever and whenever you want me to preach, I'm there. I'm your man. So, if you would please, get these goons off of me and stop allowing these wannabe gladiator guards put the heavy on me." In my finite mind, it would have seemed more justifiable if Paul was put in prison during his persecuting spree rather than after his dramatic conversion. However, God in His infinite wisdom, allowed it. And instead of being sucked in by his tornado and churning in defeating thoughts, Paul sang. He sang because of the assurance God allows and is in control of both the heavenly and the hellish times. Whether it forms from an external or an internal force, God is more than able, and willing to quiet and eliminate your tornados if you allow Him to.

The old saying, hindsight is 20/20, is so true. I have often wished I could push the fast forward button on life so I would have the advantage of 20/20 vision during a crisis situation to calm my tornado before it begins spinning out of control. Yet, since God is omnipotent and we are stuck with our finite minds, it's possible that we take the circumstances meant to give us joy and mistake them for burdens, thereby creating our own personal tornados out of them. I've told you more than you probably ever wanted to know about my tornado. Now it's time for me to get up close and personal. What's in your tornado?

Everyone has a tornado at some point in life. Some of us even experience more than a few. Take it from me, the weather may clear for a while, but if you don't prepare, that tornado will come back with a velocity so fierce, you may not be able to survive. Please don't play around for years as I did and miss the peace and true joy only He can abundantly give. Jesus wants to come into your life, quiet your tornado, and give you abundantly much more than you could ever bargain for. We may loudly protest because the picture we painted in our minds of how our life is supposed to go may look totally different from the final product. It's all about perspective. If we take one step back and get another perspective on our big picture, we can see that what we thought was a mess is actually a masterpiece in progress. Coloring inside and outside of our picture is just part of the abundant life we are supposed to experience. It has taken forty-two years for me to realize that my life is indeed the way it's supposed to be—abundantly rich in experiences.

No matter the age of a person, it's natural to mourn over opportunities that feel lost because of a disability. It feels like the right for a "normal" life has been unjustly stolen. Yet, in the right light, which Jesus Christ radiates, the abundance of experiences for someone with a disability can be joy in disguise.

To learn more, visit
https://www.writerjwalton.com.

CPSIA information can be obtained
at www.ICGtesting.com
Printed in the USA
LVHW040341021120
670425LV00003B/138

9 781953 307149